EX LIBRIS

THE BEST OF
BENN

Edited by
RUTH WINSTONE

HUTCHINSON

Published by Hutchinson 2014

2 4 6 8 10 9 7 5 3

First published in Great Britain in 2014 by
Hutchinson
Random House, 20 Vauxhall Bridge Road,
London SW1V 2SA

www.randomhouse.co.uk

Addresses for companies within The Random House Group Limited
can be found at: www.randomhouse.co.uk/offices.htm

The Random House Group Limited Reg. No. 954009

A CIP catalogue record for this book is available from the British Library

ISBN 9780091958923

The Random House Group Limited supports the Forest Stewardship
Council® (FSC®), the leading international forest-certification organisation. Our
books carrying the FSC label are printed on FSC®-certified paper. FSC is the only
forest-certification scheme supported by the leading environmental organisations,
including Greenpeace. Our paper procurement policy can be found at
www.randomhouse.co.uk/environment

Typeset by carrdesignstudio.com

Printed and bound by CPI Group (I+UK) Ltd, Croydon, CR0 4YY

Contents

Foreword

I started working for Tony Benn at the very end of 1985, intending to stay a few weeks transcribing his diary tapes while waiting to take up a 'proper job'. I stayed for twenty-eight years, and during those years edited ten volumes of diaries, managed the interconnected archive of his life's work and looked after a succession of young men and women – some still in their teens – who passed through his 'basement office' as work-experience students.

Everyone who knew Tony Benn will remember above all, I hope, his sense of fun and his irreverence towards authority. I have tried to reflect this aspect of his character in this collection through the inclusion, between the serious argument, of extracts from his diaries that show this mischievous side, which did not desert him despite periods of extreme political stress. In 1990 he and fellow MP Jeremy Corbyn slipped down into the Crypt chapel of the House of Commons armed with a Black & Decker drill, rawlplugs and screws to attach a brass plaque commemorating Emily Wilding Davison to the door of the cupboard where she hid in 1911. No permission was sought, or granted, of course, and the plaque is now part of parliamentary folklore.

A collection of speeches and articles that is intended to show the extent of Tony's interests and his mastery of communication is a challenge, not least because 'issues', as he would call them, that seemed crucially important in one period often become quickly forgotten or difficult to appreciate in another. For that reason some of the great parliamentary set pieces, such as his challenge to the Speaker over the Zircon spy-satellite controversy, and the *Belgrano*–Ponting affair, have not been included, as they would require too much contextual explanation. Conversely I have included some topics more than once, because of their importance to Tony in his own parliamentary, ministerial and social career. For example, the case he made against the European Union (as it became) was restated at different times – from the 1950s to the end of the twentieth century – as he refined and developed his arguments with each change in the nature of that political entity. Likewise his interest in industrial democracy and workers' control, and the connections between Christianity and socialism, took on different hues over the years. I have also included several biting journalistic pieces (such as one on the hanging of a prisoner in Bristol jail in December 1963) that carried a wider point or lesson. Between 1964 and 1979, when he was a Labour government minister, most of Tony's thoughtful and analytical speeches were necessarily made outside Parliament.

The chapters are arranged to mirror the main phases of his life, politically and personally, from his experience of the war as a fifteen-to-nineteen-year-old and arrival in Parliament as a young man, and his rise through the Labour Party and government; through the low years of the 1980s, when I first knew him and he seemed like a caged tiger; his rebirth as a diarist; and his later years as a widower and a loving and entertaining grandfather.

Working in Tony's office, in the basement of his Holland Park family home, was never comfortable. It was a health-and-safety-free zone, which his friends in the Fire Brigades Union would have evacuated immediately. There were burglar bars at the windows, and draughts entered through every crack. But it had a charm and a fascination for visitors and politically aware young people, with its piles of documents and rows of artefacts, all meticulously organised by Tony himself for many years. Once I started to work permanently in the 'basement office' I set these youngsters (known as the 'Teabags') the task of listing the typescripts, the Hansards, the press cuttings and the audio/video recordings that comprised the tens of thousands of items in the Benn archives, and which reflected Tony's lifetime of service to his electorate, his constituency (Bristol and then Chesterfield), the House of Commons and audiences around the world. I am grateful to Max Shanly, a trade-union-sponsored student from Ruskin College, Oxford, for all the help and advice he gave me in finding some of the extracts for inclusion in the book.

Ruth Winstone
September 2014

Introduction

In January 1940 a striking young man charged into the rooms of a very shy freshman at New College, Oxford. 'You're Butler, aren't you? I'm Benn. We are paired for Economics.' And so began a friendship that lasted seventy-one years, including thirty hours of taped interviews with me, describing his fight to disclaim the Stansgate peerage and to stay an MP. We did not agree politically but we never quarrelled as he climbed the political ladder – MP at twenty-five, Cabinet Minister at thirty-nine, hate figure in the 1970s, the longest serving Labour MP ever, and finally, for the last thirteen years of his life, a national monument, boasting that he had given up Parliament to devote himself full-time to politics.

He was notable for his energy – the two million words of his published diaries contain only an eighth of what he wrote nightly from 1943 to 2009. He spoke at endless meetings and maintained a huge correspondence. He changed the Constitution through his single-minded efforts to renounce his peerage. When Labour did achieve power in 1964 he became Postmaster General and then Minister of Technology. But as the 1960s advanced, he moved from the centre; Anthony Wedgwood Benn became Tony Benn while in *Who's Who* his entry became shorter and shorter, omitting details of his education. He emerged as the charismatic spokesman of the Left. He took the lead in opposing British membership of the Common Market and in advocating a referendum. He was one of the seven ministers to break Cabinet solidarity when the vote came in 1975, and for that he was demoted from Industry (where he had been enthusiastic for nationalisation) to Energy (where he was sceptical about nuclear power).

In the 1981 contest for the Labour Deputy-Leadership he was narrowly defeated by Denis Healey (he was delighted to point out that he would have won if the thirty or so MPs who deserted to the SDP had done so six months earlier). In 1983 he was defeated for his much-loved Bristol seat but he returned to the Commons in 1984 as MP for Chesterfield. In 1988 he made a final attempt at the leadership but was comfortably defeated by the incumbent Neil Kinnock. He continued to be active in the Shadow Cabinet and on Labour's National Executive but in the 1990s his influence waned and he was content to leave the Commons in 2001 to engage in an energetic retirement.

From his time in the Oxford Union (he was President in 1947) he was an outstanding orator. He was polite and unrancorous and always entertaining in private conversation. He was an inveterate pipe-smoker just as he was a hereditary abstainer from alcohol and a hereditary politician (he was the third of four generations of Benn MPs).

He met Caroline de Camp from Cincinnati at a 1948 Oxford Summer School and, marrying a year later, they settled for life in a large house in Holland Park Avenue. She became a distinguished educationist and her death in 2000 left a great gap in his life. They had four children and nine grandchildren. Like his father he flowered at the centre of a very close and supportive family.

David Butler

August 2014

CHAPTER ONE

Youth

*By the age of twenty-five, Tony Benn was a Member of Parliament –
the youngest MP in the House in 1950 – and a married man. Politically
precocious, as you would expect of someone with two grandfathers
and a father as MPs, he was also shy and somewhat naïve socially,
having been brought up in a family of boys and educated in all-male
institutions. In later years he reflected on the effect of these experiences
on his character. Commenting on the 1950s, he described himself
as a 'middle-of-the-road' Labour MP; but many of the concerns
that came to define his later years as a radical – security vetting,
internationalism, the honours system, the 'Europe' question (long
before the UK had become a member of the then Common Market) –
were being developed in his first ten years in Parliament and in articles
written during 1960–63, when he was banned from the Commons,
fighting the peerage case. The earliest diary entries here come from
the Tony Benn journals kept during his training as a pilot. He, along
with many other young recruits, was sent to Rhodesia to undergo basic
flying instruction; his father and brother were both also RAF pilots. At
the time of this entry Tony was nineteen.*

Tuesday 6 June 1944

I went up for over an hour and a half, during which time I finished spins and started on my final and crucial task – finding out whether I will ever be able to land an aircraft. It was not until breakfast time that I heard the great news. F/O Freeman told me the real gen. He had heard General Eisenhower's broadcast announcement to the world of an Allied invasion of the French coast, and containing the gist of issued orders to the underground movement. According to German News Agency reports, Allied landings have taken place on the Cherbourg peninsula near Le Havre and on the mouth of the Seine, reports which I heard confirmed later in the day on the BBC. It appears that paratroopers have been dropped inland to capture aerodromes and that the beach landings were effected after an Armada of 4,000 big ships, and many thousand little ones, had crossed the Channel ... a statement that besides the enormous numbers of aircraft involved we had a workable reserve of 11,000, allowing losses to that number, was given out by Churchill. At first this news made little impression on me and, had it not been for the service the Padre arranged at once, which took us all from our work at a quarter to twelve and gave us a moment to meditate on it all, this great day, perhaps the greatest day in the world's history, might have slipped by without the notice it deserved in my own mind ...

But when the workstation gathered at midday, with clerks and fitters, officers, instructors and pupils, and the air was quiet from lack of planes, and we sang 'Onward Christian Soldiers' and 'Fight the Good Fight', I thought at once of Mike and sobered up at the prospect of the dangerous work which had been assigned to

him, with the skill and courage which distinguished him from the ordinary run of pilots ...

Michael was killed on 23 June 1944, seventeen days after Tony Benn's diary entry for D-Day.

————◄○►————

My brother Michael was born in 1921, I came along in 1925, David in 1928 and Jeremy in 1935. Michael was a very thoughtful person and someone to whom I looked up with great respect, even though, like all brothers, we had fierce arguments that sometimes led to blows. Once he seized a copy of *Mein Kampf*, which I had bought when I was about twelve, and tore it apart so that, when I read it now, I have to struggle to keep the pages from flying out. He was a keen sportsman and used to row on the Thames with the Westminster Eight, which impressed me greatly.

Influenced by my mother, Michael became very religious and, when he was at school, established a prayer circle. He used to send duplicated messages, a copy of one of which I still have. A text written in purple ink on a piece of shiny paper was turned upside-down and pressed on a jelly-like substance; further copies could be made by pressing blank pieces of paper on the jelly, which then reproduced the writing in a very faint purple colour.

In 1940, when he was nineteen, Michael went up to Gorton, Manchester, where my father was then the Labour MP, but was away at the war; Mother was standing in for Father at meetings. From there he wrote to me, 'Mother is unfortunately ill and I am doing the work which she was to have done this week. Naturally I am a little apprehensive at addressing so many meetings, especially as the first one is in a church and I shall find myself in a pulpit.' He was very competent at such a young age. A few days later he wrote, 'I had quite an enjoyable time in Gorton. I spoke for about fifty minutes three times, though I was compelled to be a bit shorter on two evening meetings on account of air raids.'

Long before his death Michael had resolved that, if he survived the war, he would seek ordination and become a Christian minister, and his letters dealt at length with both religion and politics.

> Of one thing I am sure, you cannot reconcile Christianity to the war. Christ said – 'turn the other cheek', not 'go and bomb them four times as heavily as they bombed you'. Christianity is permeated with the idea of returning good for evil. All we have done is to explain that for the sake of the future, and many other things, we are justified this time in returning evil for evil. Besides this there is the other question of whether you can make up for suffering by inflicting still more and whether you gain anything anyway by adding more chaos to that which already exists.
>
> It is obviously a better thing not to fight unless there is some good reason for it, so in our case we are amply justified in doing so. The whole of our future depends on winning the war as does the future of pretty well the whole world. That is justification enough. Now I'm not arguing that the war is either justified or not justified. All I am saying is that in my opinion war is unChristian and that the church ought to say so and not compromise with public opinion.

Of course, many of his letters to me were about service life and his hopes that he would be able to qualify as a pilot, which he did, serving first as a night-fighter pilot flying Beaufighters and later on Mosquitoes.

After his tours of duty in Britain, Michael was sent to North Africa, where he shot down four German planes and was decorated with the DFC, took part in the landings in Salerno, and for a period was attached to Air Marshal Hugh Pugh Lloyd's staff.

Michael was critical of the Labour Party, based in part on the fact that it was in the Coalition and, like many people with his views, Michael took an interest in the Common Wealth Party, which, led by Richard Acland, was fighting by-elections on a socialist programme.

At the end of 1943 Michael was posted back to England and began his last tour of duty flying Mosquitoes, taking part in the famous low-level attack on Amiens Prison to liberate the prisoners held there by the Germans.

On 23 June 1944, Michael took off on a mission, but discovered when he was airborne that his air-speed indicator was not working and it would therefore be impossible to complete the mission. He was advised to drop his bombs in the sea, and another plane was asked to come in with him to indicate his air speed as he landed at RAF Tangmere in Sussex. But he overshot the runway, his plane hit the sea wall and went into the water beyond, and his neck was broken. He died later that day in St Richard's Hospital, Chichester, with my mother at his bedside, who was comforted only by the knowledge that, had he lived, he would have been totally paralysed.

Few, if any, wartime servicemen and women thought of themselves as defending the pre-war world, believing that they were fighting to prevent a return to the unemployment, poverty and militarism of the 1930s. Though Michael did not live to see it, it was those same personal convictions that were later expressed in the establishment of the United Nations and the building of the welfare state, which we then thought were objectives that made all the sacrifices worthwhile.

I greatly loved my brother Michael, and his death was a shattering blow to the whole family. The telegram arrived at the beginning of a class in Rhodesia, where I too was learning to fly. Thinking about his own life and his own ideas, I see him as a young man very much in tune with the aspirations of young people at the beginning of this century, for whom the war is a distant memory of their grandparents, although the ideas of that generation seem fresh and bright and optimistic.

My younger brother David was born when the family was in Scotland, having moved there after the Thames floods had ruined our house in London. He has always been the intellectual in the family, and was known from quite an early age as 'the professor', retaining an interest in high academic standards, which he has put to good use in his own life.

In 1935, David was suddenly taken very seriously ill with TB in his intestines, which had led to a number of lumps developing there, and we all thought he would die. Somehow he pulled through and there is no doubt that his own willpower helped. He would never allow anyone to refer to his illness and just said, if asked, that he was 'staying in bed today', showing personal courage that inspired the whole family.

It was through his doctor, a Russian immigrant to Britain, that my brother took an interest in the Russian language. He bought Hugo's *Teach Yourself Russian* and learned it by himself, encouraged but not taught by Dr Bromley on his visits. David became so proficient that when he visited the Soviet Union later, he was treated as a native Russian and was even congratulated on his Moscow accent.

When he was sent away to Bexhill and Bournemouth with Nurse Olive, the family was deprived of his company for much of the time, and to some extent the household lost its central focus because Nurse Olive had been removed.

During the first months of his illness David was taken out for walks in a spinal carriage – a long, flat, high perambulator – and used to go and watch the Changing of the Guard at Horse Guards Parade in Whitehall. The sight of him dressed up in a toy Horse Guard's uniform, gazing up at the Household Cavalry, attracted the attention of a photographer in July 1938 and a picture appeared in a newspaper above the text, 'although he may never ride a horse, he's as smart as any Guardsman with his shining helmet, breast plate and sword'.

It was not until 1938, at the age of ten, that David was able to stand, and we have a picture of him with his emaciated legs, leaning against the wall outside the guest-house where he was staying in Bexhill; it was a tremendous triumph for him that he had managed to pull through and begin to lead a normal life.

In 1935 my mother became pregnant with her fourth child and, as it was such a surprise, we nicknamed it 'the Bombshell' and looked forward greatly to its arrival. The birth was due in August, when we were all at Stansgate. Sadly, the pregnancy went wrong. Mother sensed that there was something amiss because one day the baby stopped kicking. But our doctor (who, we later heard, had been a drug addict) did not arrange an immediate Caesarian and, when Jeremy was born, he was dead. The doctor took the little body away in a white metal container, leaving us to grieve. My mother never forgot Jeremy and, more than ten years later, my father was determined to find the baby's body so that he could be given a proper funeral.

He went to immense trouble and finally located the woman who had worked in the doctor's surgery in Burnham. She remembered the incident and the fact that the baby had been buried in a white container in an unconsecrated part of a cemetery. My dad located it, managed to get an exhumation order from a local magistrate so that the body could be lifted; then another certificate allowed a cremation, and the baby's ashes were interred in the small church where my elder brother Michael's ashes had been laid and where my father's and mother's ashes are now buried.

This simple act gave my mother immense happiness and provided us all as a family with a chance to pay tribute to the baby brother we had never seen.

In a series of interviews with New Left Review, *thirty years after becoming an MP, Tony Benn discussed his immersion in Labour politics, under Attlee, Gaitskell and Wilson, between 1951 and 1964 – thirteen years when Labour was in opposition.*

After leaving the services, I returned to university eventually arriving at the House of Commons in 1950, just less than a year before the post-war Labour Government was defeated.

It looked at that time as though the economic problems that had brought such a huge Labour majority were to some extent proving to be soluble. There were shortages and other difficulties but I think a lot of people felt, and even at that stage I would have begun to feel, that the more radical socialist measures might not have been so necessary. I did not concern myself with economic or industrial matters at the beginning. In those early years I was probably a pretty ordinary, run-of-the-mill Labour MP concerned with civil liberties, with the colonial freedom movement, with libertarian issues generally and with the media – I worked with the BBC and one of my first speeches, in 1951, I think, was on the future role of the BBC. I served for ten years in the House of Commons before the peerage issue led to my exclusion. In that period I was made a front-bench defence spokesman; and in

1959 I was appointed Shadow Minister of Transport; I got involved in industrial policy for the first time in that capacity. I would have regarded myself as radical then but I did not join the Bevan Group – though I was invited to do so – because I felt that a left isolated from the mainstream of the Party would weaken its own influence.

The civil-liberties issues that most concerned me then have now become much more controversial, and indeed central, in the argument in the Labour Party. But at that time they were seen as marginal, and to that extent I was regarded as being out of the mainstream. I was not really involved in Bevan's critique of Gaitskell's Budget and the reintroduction of Health Service charges and the rest. I had a radical instinct in support of what Bevan was saying, but I did not engage in those central arguments. Even when it came to nuclear disarmament – a similarly divisive issue – my entry into it was on the grounds of public accountability rather than the straight question of unilateralism.

My first involvement was when I tried to put down a question about nuclear weapons, having discovered that the Labour Government had built the atomic bomb without telling Parliament. I was sternly rebuked by Attlee, which at that time was quite frightening, I being a new Member and he being a former Prime Minister and the party leader.

I became involved in setting up the Hydrogen Bomb National Committee (in the early 1950s). This was not specifically unilateralist; it was an attempt to see nuclear weapons as a problem of foreign policy. The campaign did not go very well: it culminated in the presentation of a petition at 10 Downing Street in December 1954. (It later led to CND.)

Gaitskell put me on the front bench in 1956 as air spokesman but I resigned a year later because I was not prepared to support the first use of nuclear weapons by Britain. My interpretation of my position would be that I was slow to see unilateralism as contributing to the anti-nuclear case worldwide, but not slow to see the importance of parliamentary control over nuclear weapons and the relationship of this to foreign policy. I did not argue for unilateralism until the Cabinet discussed nuclear weapons in 1974.

————— ‹◦› —————

A prescient speech was made by Tony in the Commons in 1956 during the Cold War at a time when the government was introducing new vetting procedures for civil servants. In it he foresaw the activities of the security services themselves, in Britain and many other countries, as constituting a potential internal threat to political freedom 'as serious as some of the external dangers against which they are intended to guard us'.

… There is a very great difference between regarding a man as unreliable because of what he thinks and regarding him as unreliable because of what he has done. My view is that, far from increasing the security of the State, if we had a lot of police enquiries, a lot of dossiers and files designed to show what men in the Civil Service have thought in the past or think now, we would be likely to encourage such great caution on the part of those civil servants that their capacity for free thought and independent enquiry would be seriously harmed and, as a result, the State would lose some of the benefit of their services. To take an exaggerated example, far from dismissing any member of the Foreign Office who had read Karl Marx, my inclination would be to dismiss anyone who had not read Karl Marx.

… Then we come up against the question of character defect and the man living with somebody who is supposed to be a communist sympathiser. [*Interruption.*] My hon. Friend forgets that if a civil servant whose wife was a communist sympathiser left his wife he might be in trouble on the ground of character defect. I think the answer to the extremists on security is ridicule. I hope that the sense of humour which is supposed to be one of our British characteristics will always prevent us from becoming too absurd in our enquiries into the views of civil servants.

… We come to the third part of the problem. The safeguarding of the free society was the first, and the second was the dangers to which we are exposed. Now we come to the methods to be employed by the government in searching out security risks. It has already been pointed out, and I think it is worth re-emphasising, that the loyalty boards are not designed in order to catch spies, but it is purely preventive work.

'Prevent us, O Lord, in all our doings' in its true sense is what the security board is designed to do. Therefore we are only undertaking all these enquiries to expose certain people who might be dangerous to us.

What happens, so far as one can make out from hon. Members who have spoken, and we all have experience of this, is that the police make enquiries to find out all about a man, all that is good, bad and indifferent. That all goes down higgledy-piggledy into the record, depending on the judgement of the man who compiles the record. It is made available to the board, which decides whether the man is suitable to be employed further or not. Then we come to the stage when the man is informed of the decision, and he has an opportunity of appealing to 'the three wise men'. Here I think there are very grave defects in the machinery provided by the White Paper.

It is argued that one cannot have an accused person interrogating witnesses because they might be doing secret work for the security forces. That might be true if a communist is confronted with non-communist police spies. At such a hearing the value of the police agents would at once disappear. But if they cannot be cross-examined by the accused himself, is that any bar to their being cross-examined by someone acting for the accused? We come back to the question of the right of advocacy on behalf of someone who is brought before the board.

Secondly, it is said that we cannot have a public trial and, in most cases, men are not charged but are brought up on suspicion. Is there any reason why a private trial should not be made more effective and more in accord with judicial procedures which we have in this country? I put these points most sincerely to the government because I believe that, when the immediate pressures of the communist world relax, sooner or later all these practices will have to be replaced by our traditional practices.

I finish with a quotation from a man who was jointly responsible for security measures in the United States with President Truman, Dean Acheson, a very distinguished American and, I believe, a very great American Secretary of State. He referred to the three presidential executive orders made in the years 1947, 1950 and 1953 which were adopted to deal with exactly this problem, and he devotes a great chapter to the problem in which he finishes with these words:

'I was an officer of that Administration and share with it the responsibility for what I am now convinced was a grave mistake and a failure to foresee consequences which were inevitable. That responsibility cannot be escaped or obscured.'

With such an authority to support me, I ask the government to look again at the White Paper, before it becomes the established practice of this country.

Two foreign policy crises dominated 1956, Suez and Hungary, both of which preoccupied and distracted Tony Benn.

Sunday 28 October 1956

To Newport last night for a conference. Harold Finch, the Member for Bedwelty, met me and took me to his home, then into the miners' welfare institute where there was a crowded room of serious-minded people. I spoke for an hour about the challenge of coexistence. It was a wonderful audience to address and the questions were good and pointed. One old boy in a quavering voice asked, 'Can Mr Wedgwood Benn tell us what value he thinks the hydrogen bomb has as a detergent?' I sat listening to the miners talking of the bad old days – the soup kitchens, the struggles with the police, the terrible hunt for work and the agony and humiliation of destitution. It was very moving and more than history – for in the crowded smoky club room were many men gasping for breath from silicosis or limping about from some industrial injury.

Today's news is mainly of the Hungarian crisis reaching its climax. The spontaneous rebellion against the communist government has virtually succeeded. The Iron Curtain has risen and people are moving freely in and out of Hungary with supplies and relief. Mr Nagy, the Prime Minister, broadcasts further concessions every hour and the red, white and green have reappeared to replace the hated scarlet banner of the communist government. Everyone in the world is breathless with hope that this may lead to a rebirth of freedom throughout the whole of Eastern Europe.

Sunday 4 November 1956

Bought all Sunday papers. Nutting, a Minister in the Foreign Office, has resigned on principle. Russia is crushing Hungary and has issued an ultimatum. A tragic, heartbreaking day with news flashes every moment that brought us all near to weeping. The last day of freedom in Budapest and the agonising goodbye to Mr Nagy in his dramatic appeal to the world. Then the Hungarian national anthem and total, total silence.

Tuesday 15 July 1958

Father had Paul Robeson and his wife to tea at the Lords. I didn't know what to expect. I wondered if he would be an embittered Red, but my doubts were dispelled in five seconds. I have never been more quickly attracted to a personality than I was to his. He is a giant of a man, towering above us all, and has a most mobile face and greying hair. He was immensely easy to talk to. You only had to mention a song of his (or of anyone else's) for him to begin singing very softly. It was just too tempting for us to go through the ones we liked best, and it was irresistible for him to sing them. I thought it might be embarrassing to have him singing in the Lords' Tea Room, but he did it so naturally and so softly that it was only properly audible a few feet away. Beyond that it must have reverberated like some Tube train passing deep beneath the building.

Afterwards I took him to the Commons Gallery for a moment and through the lobbies down to the Terrace. It was a journey of triumph. Everybody gathered round – MPs, police, visitors, waitresses from the Tea Room – for, unlike most celebrities who make you want to stare, Paul Robeson made you want to shake him by the hand. Two Negro women from Florida were almost ready to embrace him. A jet-black Nigerian was touched as if by a magic wand, and nearly split his face with a smile. You just couldn't help feeling that Robeson was a friend of everyone there. He greeted people as if he knew them, and those he really knew he remembered. There was no hint of embarrassment, whoever it was who came up. Herbert Morrison shook him by the hand on the way out and, as we marched down St Stephen's Hall, the crowds queuing for the Strangers' Gallery stood and lined the route as if it were a triumphal march.

———————— ‹o› ————————

Throughout the second half of the twentieth century and right up almost to his death in 2014 Tony Benn was developing and refining his opposition to what was known in 1963 (before Britain joined) as the Common Market of six countries and became a putative political union of nearly thirty European states. The magazine Encounter *published a series of views in 1963 on Prime Minister Harold Macmillan's first attempt to get Britain into the Common Market. Tony, who was (temporarily) excluded from the Commons after inheriting his father's peerage, was invited to contribute. He had also used a column in the* Guardian *to voice his revulsion on two pressing issues that would face an incoming Labour Government in 1964: the crisis in apartheid South Africa, and the hanging of prisoners in Britain.*

The idea of Britain joining the Common Market is emotionally very attractive. To throw open our windows to new influences, to help shape the destiny of a new community, even to merge our sovereignty in a wider unit – these offer an exciting prospect. By contrast the xenophobic, parochial delusions of grandeur fostered by the Beaverbrook press appear petty, old-fashioned, and reactionary. But the issue must not be decided by either of these emotions. A political decision of this magnitude calls for a cold hard examination by each of us of what is involved. It seems to me:

First, that the Treaty of Rome which entrenches *laissez-faire* as its philosophy and chooses Bureaucracy as its administrative method will stultify effective national economic planning without creating the necessary supra-national planning mechanisms for growth and social justice under democratic control.

Second, that the political inspiration of the EEC amounts to a belief in the institutionalisation of NATO, which will harden the division of Europe and encourage the emergence of a new nuclear superpower, thus worsening East–West relations and making disarmament more difficult.

Third, that the trading policy which the community will inevitably pursue will damage the exports of underdeveloped countries and increase the speed at which the gulf between rich and poor countries is widening.

Fourth, that on balance Britain would have far less influence on world events if she were inside than she could have if she remained outside.

Fifth, that experience shows that written constitutions entrenching certain interests and principles are virtually impossible to alter.

Of course things will never be the same again. Remaining outside means making just as many radical changes in British economic, social and foreign policy as would be necessitated by going in. But we should be free to make them in the light of the wider needs of the world as we see them.

The Common Market as it now exists is inspired by narrow regionalism. Relevant internationalism today means accepting disarmament controls, following liberal tariff and trading policies, and working all-out through the UN to end the deadly contest between East and West and substitute a policy of cooperation based on our common interest in survival. Those are the causes that inspire the new generation.

◄○►

On 13 April 1961 Tony Benn asked the Speaker for permission to address the House of Commons from the 'Bar' of the House – a small area just inside the door to the Chamber. Tony had lost his fight to remain an MP, and a by-election to elect a successor in Bristol was about to be held. The Speaker refused to let him deliver his speech. The by-election went ahead. Tony stood – and more than doubled his majority. However, as his peerage following his father's death disqualified him from serving in the Commons, his Conservative opponent, Malcolm St Clair, became the new MP. Tony was thirty-six years old, and about to lose his livelihood. This is the speech he intended to make.

Mr Speaker,

I am most grateful to you, Sir, and to the House as a whole for permitting me to attend and speak before reaching a decision on my petition. I am very conscious that the issues to be raised today are of the highest constitutional importance, as compared to which my own fate must be counted as of little importance. I shall not, therefore, weary Members with the special circumstances of my case, but will address myself to the major questions now before the House. However, I ask for indulgence to make three personal references.

First, I make no apology for wishing to remain a Member of Parliament. Service in this House of Commons is the highest service to which any man can aspire, and ought to be upheld as such. The fount of our honour is the ballot box, and it would be a bad day for this House if its Members secretly cherished a preference for the Other Place.

Secondly, I must express my thanks for the unfailing support of those who sent me to this place to represent them. Many years ago Edmund Burke, who also represented Bristol, made clear what loyalty an MP owes to his constituents. I have been sustained in these lonely months by the touching loyalty of constituents for their MP.

The Lord Mayor, Aldermen and Burgesses of Bristol have petitioned both Houses and the Great Seal of the City. Yesterday a fresh petition was presented, signed by over 10,000 of my electors. If the House made it necessary to consult them more formally, I have no doubt what their answer would be.

My third and final personal point is this. Whatever Parliament may ultimately decide about it, I am asking that the Stansgate peerage, which was created for a special purpose, having now served that purpose should be allowed to lapse completely and for all time – preserving no privileges for the future. This is the united view of the whole family, including my wife, my eldest son, my brother, my mother, and was shared by my beloved father.

I now turn to the report of the Committee of Privileges. The Committee delved deeply into the customs of Parliaments going back to 1299. In its report it chose to rest upon two very ancient precedents.

The first was the opinion of Mr Justice Doddridge in 1626 that a peerage is 'a personal dignity annexed to posterity and fixed in the blood'. The second was Mr Speaker Onslow's opinion in 1760 that 'Attendance in both Houses is considered a service and the two services are incompatible with each other'. I should like to point out that neither of these rulings have ever been laid down in Statute, nor judicially determined. From these precedents all subsequent decisions flow. The Committee did not feel called upon to 'express any view as to whether a change in the law is desirable'.

In considering the report, the House is not obliged to interpret its duties so narrowly. Indeed, the main question today is what the law should be. Is it right to endorse decisions made in 1626 and 1760 in the totally different circumstances of 1961? In the intervening years there have been fundamental changes in the composition, powers and, indeed, the whole character of both Houses.

Today the Commons, strengthened by the Reform Acts, the Parliament Acts and the establishment of universal franchise, enjoys unquestioned supremacy: where there is a conflict of duty between willing elected membership of this House and unwilling hereditary membership of the House of Lords, can there be any doubt which should take precedence?

The phraseology of the Writ of Summons to the Lords was described as being 'archaic' by the present Attorney General in evidence he submitted to a Committee of the House of Lords in 1955. The Lords endorsed this view in June 1958, when a Standing Order was passed providing that any peer who does not answer his Writ of Summons within thirty-five days shall be automatically given leave of absence for the remainder of the Parliament.

If, therefore, the Lords themselves attach so little importance to the Writ of Summons, why should this House rank it above the duties we perform as servants of our constituents? This House has throughout its history always protected its Members against those who sought to interfere with them. And in the process it has never shrunk from conflict with the Lords and even the Crown.

Does it make sense now, when those battles have long since been won, to disqualify a Member who wants to serve here and to deliver him in response to an 'archaic' Writ of Summons that the Lords do not enforce? There is here a simple contradiction between the common law and common sense. It should surely be resolved by legislation that will permit all who renounce the privileges of peerage to enjoy the rights of commoners.

What are the objections raised against this simple proposal? First, it is said that constitutional changes should not be made to suit the convenience of one person. There is no argument about that. This case must stand or fall on its general merits. Parliament did not remove the disqualification on Catholics because it liked O'Connell, or on atheists because it sympathised with Bradlaugh. It did so because it was right. The man concerned was only the occasion for change.

Secondly, it is said that this will breach the hereditary basis of the House of Lords. Yet four years ago the Life Peerages Bill provided for recruitment on an entirely non-hereditary basis, which involves far more fundamental changes.

Thirdly, it is said that this will cut off an important source of recruitment to the Lords, as if young men ritually sacrificed could somehow revitalise the ageing peers. It is an argument more appropriate to Mau Mau than to the Mother of Parliaments.

Fourthly, it is believed by some that this change would undermine the Throne itself. But such a proposition has only to be stated openly for its manifest absurdity to be apparent. It would indeed be a poor outlook for the monarchy if its maintenance were to depend on the insecure reputation and uncertain future of the House of Peers.

All these arguments and objections rest upon the assumption that our constitution is so precariously balanced on a pedestal of tradition that any change will threaten its stability. But to believe that is totally to misread the whole history of Parliament – rich with examples of brilliant innovations and studded with new precedents that have shaped our destiny.

If Mr Speaker Lenthall had been bound by tradition when Charles I forced an entry to arrest the five Members, he would not have returned his famous answer to the King asserting the supremacy of the Commons.

Our ancient pageantry is but a cloak covering the most flexible and adaptable system of government ever devised by man. It has been copied all over the world just because it is such a supreme instrument of peaceful change. In Parliament tradition has always served as a valued link, reminding us of our history, never as a chain binding us to the past. To misunderstand that would be to misunderstand everything that this House has achieved over the centuries.

———◄○►———

South Africa, *Guardian*, 17 April 1964

Of all the weaknesses that beset those in authority, blindness to reality is always the most crippling and usually the most inexcusable. Historians are merciless with 'blind' politicians – the men who base their decisions on a grave misreading of the times in which they live and who never see the great issues which are being fought out right under their noses. Historians are helped by hindsight, and hindsight is easier than foresight. So much so that some statesmen are too busy studying the lessons of the past to read the writing on the wall.

But foresight is not as difficult as it seems. The exact pattern of future events may be unpredictable, but the factors which will interact to produce these events are almost always clearly visible in the contemporary scene. Anyone who now seriously attempts to forecast world developments over the next decade can easily find all the evidence on which to base a sound estimate. And of all the developments looming up at us from the mists ahead, the outline of the coming crisis in South Africa is already the most clearly discernible.

The South African crisis has got everything. There is no great issue that is not reflected in it. It may be seen as the last stand of colonialism in the African continent. It may be seen as the nation which has most firmly entrenched human inequality and indignity into its constitution. It may be described as the most systematic police state in the world. It may be analysed as revealing the most acute class struggle since Karl Marx wrote *Das Kapital*. It may be studied as the focus of racial discrimination.

Any single one of these characteristics is full of revolutionary potential. Taken together they represent an explosive force of multi-megaton proportions capable of being triggered off by another Sharpeville or one more death sentence on a Mandela or a Sisulu. And when it starts the whole continent will be drawn in. Like Lincoln's America, Africa 'cannot endure permanently half slave and half free'. The blood that was shed in defence of that proposition a century ago will run as freely in Africa before the Sixties are out. Nor can we hope to confine the struggle to Africa alone. The world will polarise into two camps and the political fallout will drift across the oceans to poison the atmosphere wherever mixed communities are struggling to live together – even in Smethwick and Notting Hill.

What greater folly can be imagined in this situation than to fail to see it, or to see it and try not to notice it? Yet that is what this present government is doing, voting against apartheid at the UN and simultaneously supplying arms that will maintain it in force. It is just this sort of hypocrisy that reduces Britain's influence in the world. At least those who openly support Verwoerd on the basis of 'kith and kin' are honest. At least City financiers who draw an income from the diamond mines of Kimberley do not speak at Conservative rallies about liberty.

But Britain cannot stand aside or live for ever off the profits of apartheid. It is wrong and it won't work. There is no conflict here between lofty idealism and hard-headed realism. Both demand the abandonment of the shoddy acts of state that pass for a policy, and a firm national commitment to support action against the tyranny of the South African regime.

If the international law that we sought to establish at San Francisco means anything, action must be taken. This has to be said plainly if we are to understand the case for international sanctions that has been so earnestly discussed by such a distinguished international conference in London this week. It is no good dismissing its work by saying that 'sanctions are an act of war' as if that settled the argument. Sanctions may help us to avert war. But they are an act of force that amounts to a declaration of war and that is why they are right. Of course Britain cannot act alone. Nobody is suggesting that she should. In fact Britain is now acting almost alone – but on the wrong side.

It should be our job to join now with other countries to plan international action soon enough to avert the inevitable uprising. In fact, this week's conference on sanctions should be elevated to a governmental level. The earliest opportunity may come when the International Court of Justice reaches its judicial decision on the status of South-West Africa. This judgement should be enforced by an ultimatum to Pretoria backed by the threat of a total economic blockade. We must all hope that this ultimatum will be effective without the use of military force. If it is not, a UN combined operation may have to be mounted for a landing in Walvis Bay and a march on Windhoek. And, when that has been completed, a second ultimatum may well be necessary demanding the abandonment of apartheid throughout the Union and the adoption of a new constitution.

If this is what we mean to do, the sooner the South African Government can be made to realise it, the better. There will certainly be no progress until it understands that we mean business. And if we are to bring ourselves to mean business we have got to face the fact that stern action is the only alternative to disaster. If we do not see it in time, the historians will see it and wonder why we did not.

—◄◦►—

The end of the gallows, *Guardian*, 20 December 1963

On Monday afternoon the centre of Bristol was ablaze with twinkling lights and full of shoppers carrying their parcels through the jostling crowds. Every shop-window was decorated, and inside the toy departments men dressed as Santa Claus sweated under their cottonwool beards as they dispensed goodwill to the children. The record departments echoed with 'Top Twenty' discs, which now include their seasonal quota of commercial sentiment about Mary and the Christ Child. Our affluent society was busy preparing to celebrate the festival of joy and peace.

But not everyone was shopping. Outside the red-brick walls of Horfield Prison there were three twelve-year-old boys in blue duffel coats, who had come to watch something far more interesting than Christmas shopping – the preparations for an execution due to take place the next day. Why had they gone there? Why not, indeed? The hanging was the first one in Horfield Prison for ten years and it had had a lot of publicity in Bristol. For the boys this was not the flickering thrill of a TV lynching, but the killing of a real man now sweating it out a few yards away behind the high walls and who would, in twenty-four hours' time, be buried in quicklime, his death agony over. They scrutinised the faces of everyone who entered the gates. The Bishop had been to give Communion to the condemned man, who had been baptised and confirmed since his sentence. But the boys were probably waiting to see if they could spot the hangman reporting for duty. Those who believe in the deterrent value of hanging would surely have been impressed to notice how early in life it begins to exercise its awesome fascination.

Another group at the prison gates was led by a retired doctor with a white beard, his complexion made ruddy by the cold. He and his two companions were part of a long vigil which had been mounted throughout the weekend by the Bristol Campaign for the Abolishment of Capital Punishment. Leaning against the wall behind them was a simple banner inscribed with the words ALL LIFE IS WORTH SAVING. It was the only evidence that I could find in Bristol that day that the events in Bethlehem and the teachings of the Carpenter of Nazareth had made any impression at all upon our society.

Russell Pascoe is now dead. The crime for which he was convicted was a hideous one, the murder of a farmer. Why then all the fuss? One woman in Bristol wrote to ask me just that. 'Since the man awaiting execution in Horfield Prison for his part in the brutal murder of an elderly man could hardly be described as a Christian, one wonders on what grounds you base your plea that he should not be prevented from celebrating the birth of Christ by being hanged in the week prior to Christmas.' Others were more violent. A schoolgirl who stayed throughout the night-vigil described how people had come up and shouted at her. One man said: 'You're a load of ruffians. You're just as bad as the man going on the scaffold tomorrow.'

This letter and these incidents help enormously to clarify the real issue. One of the strongest arguments against hanging is because of what it does to us. The ritual revenge we take on murderers is a lightning-conductor for our own hates, a balm to ease our own guilt, and a pleasing stimulant for our own morbidity.

We reveal our advanced sensibilities by doing the killing in secret, offloading our own responsibility for it onto a hangman and a few warders whose mouths are sealed afterwards by the Official Secrets Act. Thus we are spared the painful details. We shall never know whether he fought or kicked or screamed or fainted away at the critical moment.

In the execution shed of one American prison which I visited sixteen years ago they were proud of a little device they had invented for spreading the responsibility still further. When the murderer was standing hooded and roped on the trapdoor, a signal was given to eight warders locked alone in another room. Each then pressed a different button while a spinning roulette wheel outside made its random electric contact with one of the buttons and released the catch that dropped the convict to his fate. ERNIE, the Premium Bond machine, couldn't have done it better.

How soon before the gallows are banished to join the axe, the thumbscrew and the rack, in the museum of past horrors perpetrated by man on man? Not long now. The sense of revulsion grows with every execution that takes place. The anomalies of the Homicide Act are becoming increasingly manifest. The House of Commons, in free votes, has for a long time favoured abolition. After the next election the new young MPs who will come in, from all parties, will swell that majority for reform still further. The year 1964 will almost certainly see the final end of capital punishment in Britain. This week's hanging in Bristol will probably be the last that ever takes place there.

Meanwhile the public has had its pound of flesh and we can sing our carols and eat our plum pudding free from any slight embarrassment there might have been if the execution had been fixed, for example, on Christmas Day itself. That would have been most inconsiderate.

<hr>

Monday 13 May 1963

This evening went to St Mary-le-Bow, Cheapside, for a meeting of the Christian Agnostics to hear the Bishop of Woolwich, John Robinson, talking about his book *Honest to God*, which we had gathered to discuss. The Reverend Joseph McCulloch has organised this group, justifying its name by reference to the line (from 'Oranges and Lemons') which runs: 'I do not know – says the great bell of Bow'.

At this gathering were Canon John Collins of St Paul's Cathedral, Father Corbishley (a Jesuit writer), George Dickson (an industrialist), Duncan Fairn (who took the chair), Gerald Gardiner, Dr Graham Howe (the humanist psychiatrist), the Earl of Longford, Canon and Mrs Milford, Mrs J. B. Priestley and a number of others.

The Bishop opened by saying that secularism was not basically anti-Christian and that Christians must understand and even welcome the revolt against dualistic supernaturalism, the mythological view of the world and the religiosity of the Church. He said his book was designed to help those who were in revolt to see the basic validity of the Christian message.

Canon Collins asked whether Christ was perfect, for if he was, he was then God. Woolwich replied that he wanted to write a book about Christ and that the Virgin birth made Christ seem unreal. Woolwich's interest in Christ lay in his normality, not his abnormality. He felt he could not make sweeping statements about Christ's moral life, for what was significant was his obedience. Collins replied that if you simply say Christ was 'the best man I know', Christianity could never get started.

We broke up for supper and resumed for another hour and a half. Later we had a much deeper discussion about the supernatural, in which I had a long confrontation with Corbishley about whether the evidence for the supernatural came really from external manifestations or the discovery of hidden depths. Corbishley was splendidly Jesuitical in saying that you had to have mythology 'to get people to pray'. Here is the real nub of the question. Is prayer a duty or a need?

By the summer of 1963, the Conservative government had conceded a change in the law which enabled Tony Benn to renounce his peerage, stand (again) for Bristol South East and resume his seat in the House of Commons.

CHAPTER TWO

Rising Man

By 1964, at the age of thirty-nine, and with an enormous capacity for work and a talent for communication, Tony Benn was poised to be in government. Hugh Gaitskell had just died, very unexpectedly, and Harold Wilson was Leader of the Labour Party, facing a general election in October. When the election came, Benn the modernist was given the task, as Postmaster General, of reforming the creaking old Post Office, which had hardly changed since Anthony Trollope's days; and then, as Minister of Technology, of managing Britain's industrial/ technological change (including Concorde and computers). Ten years later Tony's public speeches were increasingly concerned with the class structure and the nature of democracy in Britain, the result of his experience of the Upper Clyde Shipbuilders' work-in of 1971–2, of co-operatives and public ownership. This was at a time when the 1964–70 Labour Government's attempts to reform (or, as the trade unions saw it, to control) trade-union activity were abandoned. It was a seminal decade in his political education. Moral issues of right and wrong and the influence of Christianity also interested him particularly at this time, and continued to do so throughout his life. And in April 1964 he addressed the crisis engulfing Russia in its relations with China and America – the post-Cuba crisis – in an article for the Guardian.

The spring of 1964 may well mark the end of an era in world affairs that will rank in the history books along with the Russian Revolution, the defeat of Nazism and the beginnings of the Cold War. The events of this last week have shattered the pattern of international relationships which have shaped our thinking for the last ten or fifteen years.

By far the most significant of these events is the now open hostility between Moscow and Peking. After years of strain and tension within the alliance the differences have exploded into an exchange of abuse at the highest level. On Tuesday the *People's Daily* wrote: 'It is high time to repudiate and liquidate Khrushchev's revisionism which is leading the Soviet Union on the road back to capitalism.'

While we await Khrushchev's reply we can reflect on the comments made by Mr Gafurov, chief Soviet delegate at the Afro-Asian conference in Algiers, who said on his return through Paris: '... the Chinese want to unite the yellow and black races against the whites whoever they may be ... the National Socialist propaganda of the Chinese is not only dangerous for the Soviet Union but for all countries of Europe and elsewhere. It is hatred they are fermenting.'

Meanwhile, Senator Fulbright in a major speech in the American Senate last week attacked the 'myths' which blind America to the 'new realities' and appealed to his colleagues to 'dare to think about "unthinkable things" because when things become "'unthinkable" thinking stops and action becomes mindless'.

Fulbright argued for a complete re-examination of existing American policy towards Russia, questioning the 'self-evident truth' that 'the devil resides immutably in Moscow', towards China where 'an elaborate vocabulary of make-believe has become compulsory' and where 'inflexible policies' have 'an aura of mystical sanctity'. He even queried present policy towards Cuba and went on to say: 'In other Latin-American countries the power of ruling oligarchies is so solidly established and their ignorance so great that there seems little prospect of accomplishing economic growth or social reform by means short of the forceful overthrow of established authorities.'

In one sense there is nothing new about these Chinese, Soviet and American views. They have been developing slowly and have often been expressed privately. What is important is that they are now public knowledge and, as they are debated vigorously, all over the world they will release major new forces.

While we must all feel a sense of profound relief that the rigidity of mind and policy which we have endured in recent years is at last being broken down, there are appalling new dangers in the developing situation. We shall gain nothing from a new cold war between rich, militarily strong whites led by America and Russia and the non-white majority of the world's population pledged, under Chinese leadership, to global revolution. Yet that is just what will inevitably happen if China continues to be isolated and the basic problems of racial oppression and world poverty are not effectively tackled.

The South African tyranny, the Rhodesian crisis, continuing colonialism in Southern Arabia and the oppressive military dictatorships in Latin America will all explode in time and polarise the world into these new alignments. It will be no comfort to see

Soviet–Chinese differences erupting into frontier incidents or the breach of diplomatic relations. Nor could any sane person welcome the evolution of a Soviet–American military alliance directed against China. But these are not such very remote possibilities.

It is sad, but not at all surprising, that the present British Government has nothing useful or creative to say at this juncture. The reason is obvious. Sir Alec Douglas-Home is firmly entrenched on the wrong side of both the old and the new line-up in the world. As a committed Cold War warrior of the Dulles school, he trails far behind Fulbright in perceiving the new possibilities of an East–West détente. As an imperialist of Victorian vintage, he continues military support for South Africa, has virtually abdicated his responsibilities in Rhodesia and is currently engaged in gunboat diplomacy to retain Aden. He intensely dislikes the UN and is, at best, neutralist on the all-important racial issue. It is no wonder that this country's reputation in the world has touched rock-bottom.

Yet with a little imagination and some real faith and energy, Britain could play a most helpful role in this new situation.

1. We could take the lead in working to reunify East and West Europe, first by nuclear disengagement and later by encouraging close economic and political cooperation.

As Soviet–American tension eases there is a real chance of liberating Europe from the double straitjacket into which NATO and the Warsaw Pact have sought to confine it.

2. We should also take the lead in campaigning for a policy of justice for China: to seat her at the UN, to wind up the trade blockade and to secure the ending of American military intervention in China's foreign policy.

3. We should, both by example and through the UN, hand over the remaining European colonial possessions to their own people

and prepare drastic international action to liberate South Africa.

4. We should seek to strengthen the UN in its peace-keeping, disarmament and economic development roles, which are fundamental for the future survival of mankind.

5. We should, above all, keep lines of communication open, even through the new Iron Curtains that will soon divide us. The task of reconciliation is impossible if we forget how to speak to each other. That is what we forgot in the hard years of the Cold War and that is why the myths we are now dispersing were able to grow. We must not forget this lesson as the barrage of recrimination and abuse mounts again. The new myths – which have heavy undertones of colour – will prove far more dangerous than the old.

◄○►

The Labour Government of 1964–66 had a tiny majority, which meant that MPs were required to attend continually at the House of Commons; all-night sittings were common.

Wednesday 16 June 1965

To the House of Commons where a Mr Sheppard came to see me. He had written to me [as President of the Oxford Union] eighteen years ago asking if he could address the Union and I had written to say he couldn't, but that if he would ever like to see me I should be glad to do so. He turned up last night saying he did want to see me (about something important) and he came this afternoon. He said that he had worked for twenty years on the greatest idea ever, which he'd written down on a piece of paper. He handed me this in an envelope and, when I opened it, it said EVERYTHING

EVERYWHERE MOVES. He wanted me to take this to the Russians and the Americans so that they could share the truth equally. He was a real nutcase, but it was quite comic.

It was an all-night sitting and I simply dared not go to sleep … about five o'clock this morning Raymond Fletcher [MP for Ilkeston] collapsed in the Tea Room. It was a horrible sight to see three people holding him down and hear him groaning. Whether it was an epileptic fit, as was rumoured, or not I don't know. But this is the price we pay for such folly.

◄○►

In an interview with New Left Review *Tony Benn looked back at the reforms (published as* In Place of Strife, *1968) that Harold Wilson and Barbara Castle hoped would produce a new relationship with the trade unions. They were never implemented, opposition to them being led largely by James Callaghan in the Cabinet and by the trade-union leaders outside. Tony's dealings with Upper Clyde shipyards in the Sixties and Seventies profoundly affected his approach to industrial relations.*

The policy [of adopting *In Place of Strife*] implied two things: first, you can't run the system with full employment unless you get trade-union power under control; and secondly, a political strategy that was pure self-deception for a Labour Party: that it was possible to rise above politics and so become 'the natural party of government'. The theory was that, having won power on the backs of the trade unions, we could say to the electorate, 'We are no longer under the influence of trade unions.'

This was extraordinary, but for a time I went along with it. There were some people who knew about trade unionism, including Dick Marsh and Jim Callaghan, on the right who were very critical of the scheme. The trade unions themselves were divided about it. There were some leaders who were quite happy to see it happen because it would control their rank and file, but would not say so publicly; there were others who were totally committed against it. When we reached an impasse from which there was no possible escape except war with the movement or capitulation, I came out very strongly for dropping it. But I do not come out of that episode very well; my judgement was totally wrong and I can see now that this was the second stage of revisionism in the Party. Gaitskell had wanted to get rid of socialism by dropping Clause 4; Wilson wanted to break our links with the unions.

The opposition to *In Place of Strife* was partly that of right-wingers who had spent their lives in the trade-union movement; they were not prepared to see it crushed by a Labour Government in whatever cause; and they believed, quite correctly too, that the movement had a life distinct from the Party, for Labour would not always be in office, and there would have to be a trade-union movement in periods of opposition.

In retrospect it was a highly significant episode, which greatly humiliated the Prime Minister. The defeat of *In Place of Strife* really established that the Labour movement, when it had an absolutely fundamental interest to defend, could not be cajoled and bullied by an elected government, even a Labour Government.

Friday 29 April 1966

I had a phone call from a man in Devon. He said he had been unable to buy any 3d stamps the previous night, so instead bought 6d stamps and cut them in half with scissors and would I (as Postmaster General) authorise them to go through the post? I was helpful, but said I had no authority to authorise this and that he should have put the 6d stamp on and then written to me for a refund. Later I discovered that in fact he was a stamp dealer and had not had thirty important bills to send out – as he told me – but actually sent out 600 of these half-stamps, which he now claims are worth £15 a piece. I think he ought to be prosecuted.

Friday 29–Sunday 31 July 1966

The whole family drove off to Stansgate, arriving at 10.30 on Friday. All day doing nothing on Saturday. It takes an awful time to unwind after a week's work and I have nightmares in which I am required to see General de Gaulle about the future of Concorde, or I arrive late in the office unshaven, not having read my Cabinet papers.

An old Post Office pillar box was delivered today at Stansgate – it weighs about half a ton. I had ordered it as Postmaster General and it was to cost five or six quid. But as I had left by the time it was delivered they decided to give it to me as a gift. With a sledgehammer we broke off the bottom and gradually moved it over and erected it. I am very proud of it.

Pleasant sunny day on Sunday and we sat on the lawn. I didn't even open my red box. We drove home, getting back about 6.15. Parliament rises at the end of next week and I shall be glad of a break.

Upper Clyde Shipbuilders

My first experience of dealing with Upper Clyde Shipbuilders was as Minister of Technology in the 1966–70 Labour Government, during the period before the Tories decided it should go bankrupt. And if you want an example of the old type of state intervention, masterminded from the top, you could not have a better one than the Geddes Report and its implementation by the Shipbuilding Industry Board, which was my responsibility before 1970.

The policy ran like this: the accumulation of a number of sick shipyards into a single privately-owned shipbuilding firm; the injection into it of technocratic management, much of it from outside the industry; and of course the rejection not only of public ownership, but also of the idea that in the solution to the problems of the shipbuilding industry those who actually worked in the industry had any contribution to make. If I was educated by my experience, which is what I have tried to be, I was educated by the experience of trying it another way.

The first great example of change in the thinking of the Labour Party on this question was undoubtedly the work-in at UCS. The UCS decided to work in when the Tory Industry Minister, John Davies, told them they were ready to go into bankruptcy and collapse. Mr Heath imagined that the work-in was a little local difficulty that would quickly be forgotten. Trouble in the Clyde was not unfamiliar to Tory governments. The 'red Clydesiders', he thought, could be easily contained. But in fact the Upper Clyde Shipbuilders gave vitality to the concept of industrial democracy in a manner that we had not seen for many years. I am not saying that the UCS sit-in was about industrial democracy. As became clear, it was about the right to work. But the fact that such a campaign was linked to a demand to be allowed to continue to work, coming not from the top but from the people in the yards: that was a very important development.

As a result, the Parliamentary Labour Party adopted ahead of the Party Conference – and that's saying something – a resolution to bring public ownership to the shipbuilding industry, which was a complete reversal of the Labour Government policy in 1964–70.

During our period of opposition this was absorbed into the manifesto so that it became absolutely clear that an incoming Labour Government could not, and should not, think of its industrial policy simply in terms of what a Labour minister might do in his office, but rather in terms of a partnership between the trade-union movement and the Labour Government. That was the first step beyond the corporatist idea of public ownership planned from the top. This must be attributed entirely to what was being done on the shop floor during that period.

◄◦►

Friday 15 March 1968

Just before I went to bed I heard that George Brown had resigned and that Michael Stewart had been put in his place. So that is the end of George Brown's tenure at the Foreign Office. It began with a threatened resignation because we didn't devalue and ended with a real resignation arising out of the consequences of devaluation. What George will do now is anyone's guess. He is a person of extraordinary intellect, courage and ability, but his instability is such that it is impossible to have him in government. I wonder how capable he is of causing trouble from the back benches. His resignation now as Foreign Secretary also raises the question of his deputy leadership of the Party. It is a major political tragedy.

Thursday 21 March 1968

In the evening Caroline and I went up to Tommy Balogh's party. I had a long talk to Mary Wilson, who is very miserable, believing that if anything went right with the government in the future, Roy would get the credit and Harold would get the blame. I think she may be right as far as the press is concerned. But there's no harm in bolstering her up and I tried to.

Wednesday 3 April 1968

My forty-third birthday and the children came in with their presents in the morning, which was very sweet of them. But it was an awful day for a birthday because I had to go in very early and I was extremely tired, having been to bed so late.

Friday 18 October 1968

To Bristol and Hanham for the meeting on the role of broadcasting. The local Party had got together a few more people than would otherwise have been there. The place was chock-a-block with journalists and television people. I had been on the phone during the day and discovered that Number 10 didn't want me to comment on it on any television or radio broadcasts afterwards. Harold is obviously rather angry.

This speech by Tony Benn was the first of the now familiar critiques developed over the years questioning the power and accountability of the press, television and radio – the 'media'. Part of the speech was directed specifically at the BBC.

The BBC has assumed part of the role of Parliament. It is the current talking shop, the national town meeting of the air, the village council. But access to it is strictly limited. Admission is by ticket only. It is just not enough. We have got to find a better way and give access to far more people than now are allowed to broadcast.

The trouble is that we have extended the overwhelming technical case for having a monolithic broadcasting organisation into a case for unifying programme output control under a single Board of Governors. Broadcasting is really too important to be left to the broadcasters, and somehow we must find some new way of using radio and television to allow us to talk to each other.

We've got to fight all over again the same battles that were fought centuries ago to get rid of the licence to print and the same battles to establish representative broadcasting in place of the benevolent paternalism by the constitutional monarchs who reside in the palatial Broadcasting House.

It is now a prime national task to find some way of doing this. It must be based on, and built around, the firm framework of public service control and operation, and not dismembered and handed over to the commercial forces which already control every other one of the mass media except the BBC. For in the BBC we have an instrument of responsible communication which is quite capable of being refashioned to meet our needs in the Seventies and Eighties as it did so brilliantly in the Twenties, Thirties, and Forties.

---◄○►---

Monday 17 November 1969

At eleven, I went to the Campaign Committee, where David Kingsley presented a report on the first round of the advertising campaign for the next election, 'Labour has Life and Soul' and 'When it Comes Down to it Aren't Their Ideals Yours as Well?'

Denis Healey said we must present ourselves as a government that could govern. Jim Callaghan warned that people might not like change and might want a quieter life, which I thought was a bit of a dig at the dynamic Ministry of Technology! Generally there was a consensus and it was agreed we would do a television programme before Christmas and a party political broadcast at the end of the year, in which I would be the party spokesman.

Incidentally, *The Times* had an amusing two-column article by David Wood called 'Sandwiches with Benn'. It began by mocking me about my sandwich lunches, then said how industrialists were working happily with me and that the Tories were worried about it.

We had the Mintech [Ministry of Technology] board lunch. Harold Lever responded to *The Times* by producing some smoked salmon, freshly baked bread and cheese and some other things. It has become a bit of a joke. Next week I am going to take my sandwiches in a red handkerchief and see whether I can't lower our standards still further.

We discussed the need to ensure that there was adequate supply of stocks of fuel for winter: corrosion in the bolts in the Magnox power stations has led to a 25 per cent cutback in their utilisation, and it is potentially a great tragedy if corrosion prevents these nuclear power stations from being used at all.

————— ‹○› —————

In May 1971 Tony Benn continued his exploration of workers' control in a major speech to the Engineering Union, at the AUEW conference in Morecambe.

... One of the mistakes of the Labour Party has been its tendency to think that economic management and budgetary policy alone could get us the growth we want, or that legislation could solve the immensely complicated human relations that really determine the atmosphere in industry.

I feel this particularly strongly as a result of my experience as Minister of Technology over the four years that I spent there. We did a great deal that was useful in encouraging the reorganisation of industry, in shipbuilding and engineering, and by assisting the spread of new techniques that would help us to earn our living with less sweat and unnecessary effort.

But in one sense I became convinced that operating at ministerial level on problems of industrial organisation could be a sort of technocratic dead end. There is a limit to what you can do by mergers and public money and encouraging better management, even when you are dealing as humanely, as we tried to do, with the problems, say, of Upper Clyde shipbuilding.

What we are really looking for surely is a new approach to industrial policy that takes account of the human factor and makes our policy fit the people it is intended to help, instead of doing it the other way round. The old idea of management from the top has got to be looked at again.

It isn't only the old family business where the grandson of the founder has inherited power that he is quite unfitted to wield. The new grey-flannel brigade with their degrees in business studies, familiar with the language of accountancy and computers, and their shiny offices away from the dirt and noise of the factory floor are still often too remote, and claim too much power that they haven't the experience or knowledge to exercise properly.

I am strongly in favour of educating people in the complicated problems of organisation that have to be dealt with by upper management. There are plans to be made and long-term investment decisions that have to be got right, and big marketing operations to be mounted and a host of administrative problems to be sorted out. Without expertise in these areas a firm can easily run into difficulties or even go bankrupt.

But it is also true that the man who actually has to do a job of work on the factory floor, or in a foundry, or in a shop or office, is the best person to know how his or her work should be organised. There is nothing that creates more ill will in industry than when people are denied the elementary authority they need to plan and guide the work they are qualified to do.

One of the most horrifying experiences of my ministerial life was to walk round factories with management that obviously didn't know what was going on, or who was doing what, and yet quite happily assumed that the right to manage on behalf of the shareholders included the right to tell everybody what to do, and when things went wrong to try and find a remedy without consulting the men and women on whose work and effort the whole future of the firm depended.

I believe that there is more seething discontent in industry as a result of this situation than anyone is ready to admit. Indeed I think that many of the industrial disputes which we read about in the papers are merely triggered off by wage claims, and really reflect the deep feelings of workers who are fed up with being treated as if they were halfwits only fit to be told what to do and never asked for their advice or given the power to do things for themselves. They are consistently underestimated and their intelligence is insulted because the structure of power in industry has failed to take account of the vastly improved educational advances of recent years; and because of the fact that the mass media – with all their faults, on which I have strong views – have created a far more intelligent community than any country ever had in the whole of its history.

If we are going to talk about industrial policy let's start with the people. Let's forget about legislation for a moment and start talking about industrial democracy. And I mean industrial democracy and not just better communications, or more personnel managers, or consultations, or participation or company News Sheets. Least of all am I talking about putting one 'tame' worker on the board of a company, or trying to pretend that a few shares for the workers will make them all into little capitalists and iron out real conflicts of interest.

I am talking about democracy. And democracy means that the people ultimately control their managers. Just that, no less and no more. It's time we asked ourselves some fundamental questions about the management of industry.

For example, why should the people who own a firm control it? We abandoned that principle years ago in the political arena. For centuries the people who owned the land in Britain ran Parliament. It took a hundred years of struggle to give the people the power to choose and remove their political managers – MPs and ministers. If we can trust the country to democracy, why on earth can't we trust individual firms to the people who work in them?

This is not a particularly revolutionary doctrine in all conscience. No one is suggesting – at least I am not – that you do it by throwing petrol bombs or starting a guerrilla movement in Morecambe. You could just as easily do it by peaceful industrial bargaining and by removing the obstacles to it by legislation.

I have always thought it was a great pity that working people in Britain set their sights so low. A wage claim to offset rising prices and improve real living standards is very important for workers and their families. But if the employer passes it on by raising his prices, which the workers have to pay back to him through the shops, the gain is not always as good as it looks. Worse still, it doesn't alter the power relationship between the worker and his employer at all. Indeed, if the higher prices lead to higher profits and higher dividends, it can actually widen the gap between rich and poor and thus prop up the very system that we ought now deliberately to be trying to replace.

The trade-union movement – in both the private and public sector – ought now to develop a conscious long-term policy of negotiating itself into a position of real power in industry. Nobody can doubt the negotiating strength of the trade union movement in a modern industrial society. Indeed, the government is now underlining that power by attacking management for giving way so easily to wage claims. But why do management give way? Because they have no option. The dislocation that a prolonged strike will cause can sometimes be far more costly to the firm than paying the claim in full.

If the trade union movement were to bargain as strongly for industrial power as it does for higher wages, the management would also be ready to concede. Because then the alternative would be the high financial cost of a strike or the relatively low cost of sharing their power with the workers in their own firm.

No one could expect to achieve everything in the first year. But if the trade-union movement set itself the target of negotiating for the workers power in each firm to acquire greater control of that firm, by agreement with the present management, over a five-year period – in my opinion it would succeed.

Moreover this could be done even with the present government in power since no legislation would be needed. It might be that later a Labour Government would have to legislate to make it possible to finish the job by giving the workers the explicit right to do this.

After all, the present Industrial Relations Bill provides the most elaborate system of ballots to enforce the Tory view of trade-union democracy and provide for the recognition of agency shops and the like. What could be easier than for a Labour Government to legislate, to carry it a stage further, so that the Boards of Directors of all companies were subjected to the same procedures for ballots when they were nominated by the shareholders and could be recalled, or replaced, if they did not measure up to the job.

If we did that, many of the problems of communication in industry would settle themselves. A Board of Directors which depended for their continuation in office on the consent of their workforce would bend over backwards to communicate with them and consult them and let them participate and allow them to run their own work. They would have to.

Of course such a solution would not be without difficulties. A firm managed by consent would not find any of its problems solved by magic. It would still have to attract investment by getting a return on its capital. It would still have to find markets for its goods and produce the right products for those markets. It would still be liable to price itself out of the market by paying those who worked in it more than the market could bear. It would still need the best management it could possibly get, including the graduates in business studies. But with this one difference. They would be working, as workers, for the other workers and not for the shareholders alone.

Some trade unionists of the old school might object to this for another reason. They might fear that it would impose too great a responsibility on them and weaken their power to bargain for higher wages. But it would certainly not affect their bargaining role. They would still have to bargain about wages and conditions with the management the workers had chosen, just as they now have to bargain with the managers that the shareholders have imposed on them. After all, the electors still bargain with a government even when they have elected it.

But it is true that this bargaining would be done under conditions in which the workers had to share the responsibility for the consequences of the increased wages they were asking for and everything else they did.

Indeed, one of the most powerful arguments for adopting the policies that I am discussing is exactly that *responsibility* would be placed upon workers in industry who already have *massive* power but are now denied the responsibility that should go with it. The third industrial revolution has transferred this bargaining power to the workshop, but the legal structure of our companies has not been adapted in such a way as to allow this responsibility to go with this new power.

For the community as a whole, a policy for industrial democracy could help to combat inflation and increase productivity. Wage claims that might really bankrupt the firm would obviously not be pressed in a firm where self-management had placed the ultimate responsibility on the workers. And if the workers in a firm could be given the power to plan their own work, to take account of their own skills, productivity might increase more rapidly than could ever be achieved by hiring hordes of management consultants, to tell the managers to tell the workers what to do in the interests of the shareholders.

But this alone would not be enough. It might – and I believe it would – provide the outline of a practicable sensible alternative to the short-sighted and reactionary Industrial Relations Bill now before Parliament.

But what it would not do would be to solve another equally difficult problem of the unacceptable differential between the highest-paid directors in any company and the really low-paid workers whose incomes are an affront to a society that pretends to be civilised.

It is true that the problems of differentials would certainly be discussed in any firm that had adopted self-management. But the percentage system by definition continually increases differentials again. 10 per cent of £15 a week is very different from 10 per cent of £20,000 a year and nothing that we have yet thought up, by way of national machinery, or ministerial intervention, offers us an answer to that problem.

It may well be that we have been looking at the problem from the wrong angle. It might be better to re-examine it from the point of view of the firm itself, since it is the firm which earns the income for everybody who draws his salaries or wages from that common pool. It is clear that if those at the top draw too much out of that pool there will be less for those at the bottom. The moral responsibility for seeing that those at the bottom get an adequate income must surely rest squarely and fairly on those others who draw a bigger income from the same pool.

If this is so, then it is the ratio between the top salaries and the bottom wages in each firm that ought to interest us. Suppose, just for example, we set this ratio at 10–1. To take one case: suppose we laid it down that if the lowest wages in a firm were £15 a week – or £750 a year – then the highest salary paid should not exceed £7,500 a year. 10–1 is a very wide ratio, but there are thousands of firms – if not the overwhelming majority – where the lowest-paid do get £15 a week and the directors get £10,000, £20,000 or more, which is not ten times as much, but twenty or thirty times as much.

So far I have not dealt with public enterprise. It is a sad reflection on the way in which we have set up our nationalised industries that, even in those industries, we have got nowhere near real industrial democracy, nor achieved any fairer distribution or incomes between the board members and the lowest-paid. So if the policies which I have been discussing were only applied in the public sector, it would do more to change their social purposes and working environment than the act of nationalisation itself.

But there is no reason why we should not get exactly the same benefits even in firms that are privately owned. The shareholders could be contained into their more limited role, as investors, free to move their money in and out, but deprived of their present insupportable and unenforceable claim to be the sole arbiter of the fate of the workers in the firms they own, or the sole authority to whom the management should be responsible.

What then is the case for the extension of public ownership? Clearly if by industrial democracy, and an egalitarian incomes policy, we could drive capitalism back into a more limited role, as a form of investment deprived of the power that has historically gone with it, the argument about public ownership changes its character. But that is not to say it loses its force.

Quite the reverse. One thing should certainly be clear from our experience of the last Labour Government – and perhaps nobody is better qualified to say it than I am, because I was responsible for administering the policy. Never again should a Labour Government pour money into private industry without claiming, and acquiring, the same rights as any other private investor in exactly the same proportion as the total public investment stands to the private investment.

If we had done that in the last Labour Government, many of the firms that we helped – certainly in shipbuilding and in the aircraft industry – would have automatically moved into the public sector simply by virtue of the grants and loans we made available. It would have been better to have done it that way. Next time we should see this as a conscious and constructive approach to the extension of public ownership.

After the Tories have first bankrupted, and then nationalised, and then subsidised Rolls-Royce, we would certainly have nothing to fear from their opposition to such a policy in a general-election campaign. Indeed, I think the whole public attitude to public ownership has undergone a fundamental change and there is far more widespread support for it than there was even a few years ago.

And if nationalised industries were seen to be democratically run, and to be distributing incomes more fairly as well as being accountable to the public for the major decisions they make, we could take a massive step towards democratic socialism. And we could do it by the traditional means of common sense and public consent which lie at the hearts of the traditions of parliamentary democracy and the British Labour movement.

———◄○►———

The master illusion of British politics was a speech made in early 1974, at the same time that Parliament was dissolved for the unexpected General Election of February 1974, and provided Tony Benn with an opportunity to link the election issues to the class structure of our society and the illusion of British politics that denied the existence of those divisions. It identified the main task of the Labour Party as defending working people and their families and the trade unions, and warned of the dangers that a corporate state might emerge if Edward Heath succeeded. It also listed six Establishment tests by which all political leaders were to be judged and that constituted the essentials of Conservative thinking, and ended with a quotation from Clause 4, whose relevance was now so obvious. The inconclusive February election was followed by a second in October 1974.

Thursday 10 October 1974

Polling day. To Bristol Transport House, where the *Daily Mirror* was waiting – they photographed me at a couple of polling stations and on top of the car with my loudspeaker.

At one o'clock we had lunch and I made a further thermos so I could drink tea from my tin mug while sitting on top of the car. The seat was so hard, I got really sore. Fortunately, there was very little rain but it was cold up there and I had my anorak and blanket round me.

Josh arrived in the afternoon. He and Stephen went around together all afternoon and were terrific. We worked right through, had a cup of tea with George Easton, then finished at about 8.45 and went back to the hotel for a meal.

The results began coming in. The polls this morning were showing on average a 5.5 per cent Labour lead, but it became quite clear that this distribution of our lead varied very much according to which part of the country it was, and in the Tory marginal, where they were fighting like hell, they did actually manage to hold their own. The computer began by predicting a sixty-six overall majority, but it narrowed and narrowed as the night went on.

To the count at about 12.10. BBC and ITN television said that mine was the only result they intended to show from the South West, and when I asked all the Labour agents who were gathered in the classroom, which we had booked and provided with a kettle, milk, teabags and sugar, there was an overwhelming vote against letting the cameras in to the declaration. ITN and the BBC were extremely angry. The result came out at about 1.15 a.m., a great deal earlier than in the last election. My majority was 9,373 compared with 7,912 in February. I had a 17.7 per cent majority and my percentage of the vote rose from 47 per cent to 49.1 per cent. It was an absolutely superb result.

I went back to the hotel and watched the results until about 4 a.m. The computer prediction was of a Labour majority of five by the time I went to bed. In the event it was three.

Saturday 19 October 1974

Frank McElhone rang, shocked by Keith Joseph's speech in Birmingham, and saying that it would thoroughly upset the Catholic Church. Joseph's speech on 'The remoralisation of Britain' was an attack on permissiveness on the Mary Whitehouse model, and had advocated birth control for poor families so as to reduce the number of children they would produce, since the mothers were unfit to look after them. It was a complete master-race philosophy; the theory that the problem is the immorality of the poor, rather than poverty, is a most reactionary idea bordering on Fascism.

————◄◦►————

The crisis situation which is developing in Britain as a result of the Prime Minister's decision to seek a confrontation with the miners is quite different from anything that has happened within the lifetime of most of us.

The next few days, while the miners' ballot is taking place, and before the result is known, offer us all an opportunity to analyse the elements of this crisis and to reflect upon it, before events take charge ...

Working people are becoming aware of the consequences of Mr Heath's counter-inflation policy, which is deliberately designed to bring about a substantial redistribution of wealth and income in favour of capital at the expense of Labour.

It is, indeed, obvious to everyone that even the developing discussion about pay relativities is being confined to the relationship between the wages of higher- and lower-paid workers – without dealing, at all, with the wide and growing gap between the richest people, on the one hand, and working people as a whole, on the other.

This is why, in the long run, Mr Heath cannot win. There is no immutable law of economics or nature – no 'Iron Law of Wages' – which requires working people to be treated as a separate class, allowed only to compete amongst themselves about who is to get most from a fixed proportion of the national income allocated to them in wages by those with wealth and power, who regard the differential between themselves and working people as a whole as being naturally exempted from public discussion.

It is the absurd injustice of this system that has begun the first serious public questioning that has taken place in this country, about the total distribution of wealth and income, for very many years.

In short, our class structure is at last being publicly examined. Questions of class have not been properly discussed for over a generation.

Yet the reality of class privilege, and class deprivation, remained and was understood and accepted by all classes, even if only as an undiscussed and undiscussable fact of life, reflected in the type of housing people had, the wages they received, the educational opportunities afforded to their children, extending right throughout their working life to the two nations in old age.

When historians come to write about this period of British history Mr Heath will certainly be credited with having awakened people, who had never thought about class before, to what class means, and how it relates to their own experience. This will greatly increase support for the unions and the Labour Party, and it explains why the people are rallying to the miners now.

The Conservative Party has already become uneasily aware of the dangers for it of Mr Heath's own action in awakening class consciousness by his policy of confrontation.

The very existence of the Conservative Party, the alliance of forces that make it up and its appeal to workers in an election depends upon the denial of the existence of class divisions in British society.

The Conservative version of national unity rests upon the creation of an illusion that the rich are kind and that, if only working people would be restrained, we could all raise our living standards together, in an unending bonanza of capitalist growth fuelled by some 'necessary' inequalities to provide the profits mainly needed for investment.

That is the master illusion of British politics.

If we cling to that illusion we shall condemn ourselves to a continuation of the present sterile stalemate in British politics. Destroy that master illusion and the democratic reform of our savagely unjust society becomes possible.

This is why the Labour Party in its manifesto argues for 'a fundamental and irreversible shift in the balance of wealth and power in favour of working people and their families' through the ballot box and parliamentary democracy, which our forefathers fought for and won.

Labour's main task in the next few weeks is to defend those whose living standards are under attack; and to protect our basic democratic rights.

For it is clear that Mr Heath has decided that the preservation of the existing pattern of power and privilege must be maintained, and he has shown himself ready to do so, even if it means dismantling the traditional democratic structure of the trade unions, local authorities and Parliament itself – and attacking the democratic traditions within the Labour Party itself.

The legislation on industrial relations, rents and the Common Market was passed for that purpose.

The Conservative Party, and their allies, including the mass media, are prepared to sacrifice even free enterprise itself in order to preserve the pattern of power and wealth that corresponds with their class interests.

This is why they are moving towards an industrial system with some features drawn from corporate states.

This is also why the Establishment has developed six acid tests by which all political leaders are to be judged, before they can be supported by editors and television and radio commentators.

These tests are as follows:

1. Uncritical support for British membership of the Common Market.
2. Full backing for the Industrial Relations Act.
3. Belief in a statutory wages policy.
4. Opposition to the links binding the trade unions to the Labour Party.

5. Hostility to the democratic role of the Labour Conference in the policy-making of the party.

6. Denial of the existence of class as a factor in British politics.

Loyalty to these six principles is now seen as essential for survival by those who control our society.

It is exactly these principles which stand in the path of working people as they seek to safeguard their interests.

It is against this background that the Labour movement must now – this very week – take up its historic task again.

It is for us to tell the nation clearly that we are committed to the political, social and economic emancipation of the people, and more particularly of those who depend directly upon their own exertions by hand or by brain for the means of life.

In the early Seventies Tony Benn gave a lecture on 'multinationals and world politics' at a conference of business leaders in Trinidad, soon after he had visited China. It identified a number of international, national, trade-union and political forces that would need to be deployed as a countervailing power to check the abuse of power by the multinationals. It was somewhat coolly received!

… The nation state at present offers the only scope for popular influence to be brought to bear on the political and economic power of business.

During the Sixties the growth of multinationals was in many cases more rapid than the growth of national budgets by which governmental power may be measured and, in the UK, the profits of the multinationals have been higher than those of purely domestic enterprises. This suggests that the powers of the multinational companies are most likely to grow and to find themselves more and more the subject of political interest as the years go by. In particular trade-union interest, expressed directly and indirectly through the political system, is likely to be a bigger factor in shaping governmental responses.

Looked at globally, the concentration of industrial technology in the north is now one of the major political factors in the world today, as may be seen by comparing the growth of production in the northern hemisphere with the growth of population in the south. This distorted development pattern complicates the relations between the white and non-white races since it deepens the ethnic division of which we have become increasingly aware in recent years. And since the multinationals have played a part in that pattern of development and operate worldwide, they are seen as a symbol of northern domination.

The first concern of governments in dealing with multinational enterprise lies in the area of industrial and economic policy, where the multinational has a built-in advantage deriving from its international status, permitting it to escape more easily from domestic legislation of all kinds by planning its own development in a way that best suits its own interest, undertaking new investment to take advantage of lower labour costs, lower taxation, easier labour relations, and even to avoid domestic regulations governing pollution or measures to locate industry to meet the regional policy of national governments.

Although the differences of ideology between the capitalist and communist halves of the developed world have dominated political thinking since the Cold War began, it is now apparent that this division may have less significance than the tension growing up between the developed world as a whole and a Third World which sees itself challenged by both capitalist and communist superpowers spreading their influence southwards, by both military and industrial pressures.

The recent emergence of China has acquired greater significance just because its whole world strategy seeks to marshal the Third World against – as she sees it – American imperialism and Russian social imperialism, by spreading revolution.

It would be a mistake to think that the only effect of technological development has been to create very large organisations of which military establishments, multinational companies and big governments are the most obvious examples, and that all that needs to be done is to adjust people's attitudes to accept those developments and learn to live with them.

Higher living standards, better education, access to news information and a variety of cultural and ideological influences through the mass media have expanded the horizons of the world's population in a way that no one could have anticipated fifty years ago. This in its turn has triggered off tremendous new movements by ordinary people to expand their scope and improve their opportunities and environment. The anti-colonial movements, political revolutions throughout the world, the struggle for racial equality and human rights, women's liberation, a cleaner environment and the revolt against materialism are all part of the same process that produced the global corporation. Moreover, in the process people have acquired far greater power to enforce their will because an interdependent economy and society is much more vulnerable to direct pressure. Strikes, hijacking and urban guerrilla movements each in their own way illustrate the extent to which real power has been distributed downwards as well as upwards, by the process of technical change.

The effect of all these developments has been to outdate many of the political institutions that we have inherited from the past.

Fifty years ago all the effective political and economic decisions were taken within nation states which were only subject to occasional external military pressures.

Today the pattern of institutional development has begun to change radically. Some functions of the nation state we have attempted to transfer to the world level. Others are dealt with by regional organisations like the Common Market, involving many nations.

Similarly most governments have devolved more powers from the centre downwards, and every political system is being subjected to growing pressure from underneath, from people who want to have a greater say over their own future.

This new pattern of world institutions, now embryonic in character, could – if further developed – be made strong enough to contain and absorb the power of global corporations. We still lack a clear idea of how this framework will operate. But the need for it is becoming more apparent.

The necessary framework within which global corporations should operate will have to be constructed at various levels from the United Nations right down to plant level.

The internationalisation of industrial technology has now proceeded so rapidly that it is not unreasonable to expect that the UN – set up to prevent the misuse of military technology by war – should extend its functions to take on board responsibility for supervising some aspects of the operations of global companies which are of international concern.

What may well be required is something approaching the diplomatic recognition of these companies, when they reach a certain size, holding them accountable directly to the UN for any decisions that they make, which affect international peace and security or human rights.

With all its imperfections, the UN is the only international centre of political representation to which these international companies could in any way be made accountable. For example, it could be that the quickest way to bring sanctions to bear on a particular country would be by laying down an international embargo enforced through control of international companies.

The registration of the multinationals with the UN could carry with it the requirement to supply information about their activities on a regular basis, and might offer some measure of protection for their legitimate interests, if these were improperly threatened.

There is also scope for the development of ground rules which will make possible an expansion of industrial operations between the Western and communist world, and the developing world. We shall soon see more international companies operating within the communist world. There will also be joint ventures that will bring the big communist industrial organisations increasingly into the non-communist world, which will require that they should be regulated too. The 1970s could well see communist multinationals emerge in competition with those from the capitalist countries.

The attitude of national governments towards multinational companies necessarily reflects their interpretation of the national interest, which they were elected to safeguard, taking account of all the external and internal influences to which they are subject.

The nation's economic performance, seen as a whole, is a major priority in all countries, and global corporations will be judged by their contribution to it.

There may also be strategic considerations or matters of national pride which make it undesirable that the control of a key industry should fall into foreign hands.

Moreover the attitudes of the community towards business generally, as reflected through trade-union and other social pressures, will reflect themselves through the democratic process in such a way as to influence governments in their policy-making.

In Britain, policy towards multinationals has evolved in recent years, based on an understanding of their value in bringing inward investment, new technology, management skills and access to world marketing operations. In addition, Britain herself has a number of large and important home-based multinational corporations which are important export earners – both visible and invisible.

Perhaps the most important development of government policy has been the decision to engage in direct consultations with big companies seeking information on a reciprocal basis. Governments have wanted to know about the inward and outward flow of trade and investment, transfer pricing practice, the extent of access by British subsidiaries to export markets, managerial devolution, industrial-relations practice and research policy, and have sought to win the support of the multinationals for the location of new plant in areas of high unemployment. The multinationals have wanted information about all government policies that affect their operations or plans.

All this amounts to a form of diplomatic recognition, followed by negotiation to identify the areas of common interest and the possible areas of conflict.

In these negotiations the balance of power between the two sides has been a subtle one. The global corporations are clearly dependent upon the maintenance of the goodwill of the host country, their own general reputation, the need to safeguard their own investment and even the importance of such non-economic factors as the national loyalty of their UK employees. The government, for its part, knows of the potential power of these companies to move elsewhere if the going gets too rough.

The trade unions operating nationally and internationally can bring pressure to bear on their governments, and on international organisations, to develop policies and procedures that will safeguard their interests.

The unions in Britain have underlined the need for a more systematic collection of information, for conformity with British industrial-relations practice, for the need to develop increased consultation between the companies and the unions on corporate planning, including manpower plans and research policies. These pressures have already reflected themselves in British Government policies and are likely to increase in the future.

There has also been a slow but steady development of international trade-union links, which may tend progressively to redress the balance – or at least part of it – between capital and labour.

But it may be that, at the plant level, we shall see the most significant changes over the years. Here there is a combination of pressures from management for the devolution of real responsibility and parallel pressures from workers for a far greater say in the control of their working lives.

These trends may be regarded as a part of the development of personnel policies designed to increase involvement or job enrichment. For workers' participation merges imperceptibly into a demand for industrial democracy. The pace of advance towards this objective, and the extent to which it moves towards true worker self-management, will depend partly on the attitude of management itself and partly on the development of political ideas in the working-class movement generally.

Companies faced with these demands will, in my judgement, be bound to respond to them partly in the interest of efficient operation and partly because of their vulnerability to pressure from below. It was exactly by conceding to pressures from below that political, industrial and social advances were made throughout British political history, and which explains the combination of change with stability of which Britain is most proud.

It will be clear from this line of argument that the future of the multinationals is inextricably bound up with the development of world politics, and cannot be isolated from main currents of political thought.

The mythology which the multinationals have sought to develop to justify their own existence is a mythology that is bound to come under challenge in the new era of world politics which we are just entering.

Most global corporations grew to their present strength at a time when the United States was the unchallenged, and unchallengeable, political and military power in the world, and when American business philosophy was enjoying a pre-eminence sustained by this political and military power.

But in the Sixties this pattern of American pre-eminence has been challenged by the growth of alternative centres of power, first in the USSR, then in Japan and Western Europe, and now by the emergence of China.

It will no longer be possible for those who run the multinationals to avoid entering into political alliances, with all the compromises that this may involve, if they are to survive.

But the more political they become in order to survive and expand and advance, the more they must expect to find themselves subject to political pressures exerted upon them by nation states and international organisations.

In short, multinational companies employing thousands of people, controlling great resources, with a vested interest in territorial development and with reserves of capital and know-how to protect, have become states and must expect to be treated as such.

Like all states, they will be subject to the demand for political and democratic control. If this is not successfully achieved, many of the advances that the West claims for political democracy, as compared to centralised bureaucracy or dictatorship, could be eroded, until the main difference between the systems finally disappears.

This is the biggest political challenge facing man in his attempt to control his own environment. For having developed an engineering capability which allowed him to conquer nature, he finds he has set up organisations that may in fact control him.

The single biggest political issue of the Seventies, Eighties and beyond is the need for democratisation of power.

In communist countries, this must necessarily mean gaining real popular control over the bureaucratic structure of the State and dismantling its most dictatorial features.

In the West, it must involve the democratisation of political bureaucracies, military machines and industrial power symbolised by the global companies.

In the developing world, it must mean a determination to shape their own individual destiny without falling under the military influence of the superpowers or the economic control of multinational companies.

To succeed, global industrial development must therefore recognise the inevitability that it, too, will have to adapt itself to accept democratisation. If it does not do so, it is likely to go the way of all authoritarian systems.

―――――◄○►―――――

As one of the great communicators of the twentieth century, and indeed a consummate exploiter of the media generally, Tony Benn had an ambiguous relationship with broadcasting and the press. His clashes in later years on live television became legendary. At a Manchester

University symposium in the early 1970s he set out the relatively modest case for reshaping broadcasting in Britain 'to allow it to be used more fully by the people'.

It is impossible to separate broadcasting policy and the influences which shape it from the other information-disseminating systems in society, and the restraints under which they operate.

The whole political process in a democracy rests on the maintenance of a delicate fabric of communication within society, which reveals the common interest that exists, identifies conflict where it arises, and painfully builds the consent which leads people to accept the policies that emerge as these conflicts are resolved, by upholding the ground rules of the system.

Similarly the whole educational system is an information-disseminating system passing wisdom from generation to generation, sustaining and reflecting the inheritance we have acquired from the past and bringing human genius to bear on the problems of society in such a way as to allow mankind to adapt itself more easily to the changes that are occurring, and to anticipate future events as they loom up on the horizon. Legislation governing the educational system and its accepted value structure have shaped its pattern.

The media are engaged in the same process and are so much more effective in disseminating information simultaneously to large groups of people that they not only supplement the political and educational systems, but in some respects supplant them, because of their enormous power. But they do so without the restraints that have been built into the political and educational systems over the centuries. The tension that is building up between the media, politics and education arises in part because we have not yet developed a framework of public responsibility expressed through external influences within which the media can operate so as to maximise their value and minimise the dangers that must necessarily follow from the irresponsible use of so much power.

Examples of this tension can be found in every country in the world. A series of arguments in Britain – too well known to need repeating – between political leaders and the broadcasters culminated in the recent clash between Westminster and Stormont ministers and the BBC which highlighted the problem in a most vivid way. The sustained attack by Vice President Agnew on the American television networks has headlined the same problem in the US. The role of the mass media in accelerating the liberalisation in Czechoslovakia during the Dubček period, thus contributing to the Soviet decision to intervene militarily, offers an interesting example from the communist world.

Similarly the anxieties being expressed worldwide about the effect of violence and sex on television, as a corrupting force undermining the traditional role of the educational system in preserving cohesive social values within society, indicates a growing suspicion that the influence of television may be greater than the influence of schools in shaping the whole character of our people.

These questions are far more important than the subject most usually raised by politicians and broadcasters in public debate – whether or not the mass media are fair to the political parties and individual parliamentary leaders. Since everyone suspects that any politician talking about the media is likely to be motivated by discontent at the way politicians are treated, I should like to make it clear that this is not the basis of my comment, and I am not advancing any argument for controlling the mass media by government in the interests of political leaders.

The nub of the political system in Britain is, and always has been, its twin capacity, first to secure free debate, secondly to give an expanding electorate progressive power to select its participants in that debate through the extension of the franchise.

Long before Parliament – the talking shop – was in any sense democratic, it had a creative and positive role in probing the exercise of power by kings and landowners and it opened up policy for public examination and acted as a safety valve for public discontent. Later, as the vote was extended to more and more citizens, the representative character of MPs was enlarged and the right of selection of those MPs by the public was the basis of this process of the democratisation of power.

Thus the exercise of power in the political system is governed by some very important constitutional statutes, such as the Parliament and Representation of the People Acts, operating as an external restraint, and the common-law developments described in the parliamentary bible, *Erskine May*, which provides the ground rules of the system. In the House of Commons itself the choice of speakers to be called is regarded as so sensitive a matter as to require the discretion to be exercised by the Speaker, a man who separates himself from all party loyalties as a price he must pay for winning the trust of the House.

By contrast, the mass media operate under very different restraints that have grown up only in the past fifty years and which provide for broad political balance, but very little else. The choice of people to broadcast, and be given access to the public greater even than an MP can hope to aspire to, is regarded as the proper function of the producer of the programme, who is himself appointed by the BBC or ITV company on the basis of his abilities, as revealed to his employers.

Nor is there adequate provision for the judgement exercised by the broadcasters to be called to democratic account. In the case of independent television there is the ITA, a licensing body with some power over the companies, including the right to disallow programmes and ultimately to grant or withhold the licence to continue broadcasting. In the case of the BBC, the Board of Governors – themselves influenced by outside comment – sit in judgement on their own employees and, whatever complaints procedure they may institute, they are still judging their own case.

Moreover, the governors of the BBC and the ITA are both appointed by the government of the day, and just because of the potential power this gives to the government, it normally bends over backwards to avoid exercising its power and leaving itself open to a charge of censorship.

As compared with the parliamentary system of communications, the system as operated by the mass media is therefore seriously defective and inadequate, in that it is basically undemocratic and there is no accountability of power.

This poses a major challenge to those who are thinking about the future of British broadcasting. Nobody wants governmental political control, but the present combination of corporate or commercial control, theoretically answerable to politically appointed boards of governors, is not in any sense a democratic enough procedure to control the power the broadcasters have.

What is required therefore is some way of developing a new framework to democratise this power, without falling into the trap of state control or confusing commercial competition and free-enterprise control with the free expression of different views on the air.

Undoubtedly, as technical developments proceed and the number of channels increases, either by air transmissions or by the development of multi-channel coaxial cables, the problem will get easier rather than more difficult. But even here there will be problems of accountability to be faced, which may need to be worked out well in advance.

One method of democratisation worth further exploration would involve an external attempt to democratise the internal structure of the broadcasting organisations, so that the actual production units had a greater say over their own output, but were collectively held fully accountable to those outside for the use they made of that freedom. I am not referring to the producers alone, but to the whole team including directors, studio managers, scriptwriters, cameramen, sound recordists, technicians, secretaries and other workers.

If these discrete units could be identified and democratised so that they discussed their own policy and output, the men in charge within them would be accountable to their own subordinates and colleagues, and external complaints about the programmes they put out would then also have to be discussed within the same democratic framework. This is the way of industrial democracy or workers' self-management and although it must sound strange or foreign, or unrealistic or alarming, to those brought up in the hierarchical traditions of British organisational practice, it has great potential and is well worth serious consideration.

Those complaining of unfairness would thus be directing their complaints, initially, to the whole team that made the programme, and the whole team would have to agree on its response, and in the debate that ensued there would be pressure from inside to change policy where this seemed necessary. Moreover, everyone involved would be forced to accept his responsibility for the output of the unit of which he was a member.

At the moment those working in broadcasting can very often slough off their responsibility by pointing out, quite accurately, that the responsibility for the conception and execution of the programmes upon which they are engaged has nothing whatsoever to do with them. There is, in short, no code of conduct accepted by broadcasters as a whole.

The second road to democratisation involves a fresh look at the whole question of access to the media, which has been debated with growing intensity over the past few years.

It is, on the face of it, quite absurd that only the BBC and the ITV companies should have any say on who should appear on the air and what subjects should be discussed. It is as if the ownership of a printing press was the only means by which anyone could get anything published, unless he could persuade somebody else with a printing press to accord him this right.

The publishing function has been very largely neglected until recently and almost the whole output on all channels has been devised and presented under editorial direction. This has had serious political consequences. Since those with something constructive to say, together with others expressing discontent in society, have been denied the right to 'publish' their views, some important grievances have festered until they reach explosion point. And when the explosion comes, the mass media have been only too ready to give extensive coverage to the demonstrations and violence that resulted and to pontificate endlessly *after the event* on the reasons why things had gone wrong.

What they should have been doing was to provide ample time for these views to be expressed beforehand, so as to provide society with the feedback essential to correct its errors before they do too much damage, and the chance to understand future choices by having the alternatives presented to them.

The arguments used against giving access have been various, and it is worth examining some of them to test their validity.

First, it has been argued that there is no time available for this purpose and that if an attempt was made to provide it, the public at large would be bored and would switch off.

But are we to accept the ratings as the final determinant of what should and should not be broadcast? The BBC, though financed by the licence and not by advertisements, is subject, through competition, to exactly the same pressures as commercial companies and therefore demonstrates in its output no greater evidence of public responsibility.

Some cultural minorities are well catered for. What is evidently not accepted is that the minority who are really interested in a penetrating study of social problems – industrial relations, race relations or Ulster – are equally entitled to have access to the information they need to help them form a judgement.

Secondly, it is also argued that the problem of selection of groups and individuals to whom access should be given poses impossible difficulties for those who would be called upon to make a choice between them.

There are difficulties, but they are not insuperable, and many of the groups to whom access should be given are self-selecting because they represent important interests in the State that are capable of throwing up their own representatives through their own internal selection processes.

For example, the televising of Parliament would involve giving Parliament direct access to the people, by allowing the cameras to observe what happens there. The fault here lies with Parliament and not the broadcasting authorities, and it no doubt soon will be resolved.

Similarly the trade-union movement, with its enormous national membership, should certainly be entitled to its own regular programmes showing its policies to the public.

Industry, too, could legitimately lay claim to its right to direct access. The discontent so forcibly expressed by so many trade unionists at the way in which industrial issues are handled by the media is exactly matched by the discontent felt by industrialists, many of whom greatly dislike television coverage of their problems.

The professions, too, could properly claim to talk directly about the subjects on which they are most qualified to speak, and so could different regional authorities which represent important areas of the country, who feel that they have been improperly treated by the community as a whole.

Then there are the thousands of pressure groups representing racial minorities, special interests and a host of other concerns that at present depend solely on the possibility that they may be invited to contribute a speaker to a discussion that has been set up by a producer to fill a slot in his schedule.

It is said that these subjects are already dealt with in regular programmes or schools programmes or special features. These should obviously continue, but there is all the difference in the world between a programme devised by a producer and a programme presenting the considered view of a group that has something to say and is entitled to be heard.

Thirdly, it is argued that the intervention of a professional communicator is necessary because ordinary people are so inarticulate and cannot be relied upon to express themselves clearly. But most people are very articulate when they are talking about what they know best.

The argument for wider access has already gained substantial ground in recent years, and there are now some examples which can be cited to illustrate how it would work.

Quite apart from the Dutch system, which has aroused some interest in Britain as part of the argument over the fourth channel, there are some domestic examples worth noting.

The recent Ulster programme itself offered a very interesting case-history and was one of the most important developments in the use of television in public affairs that we have seen in this country.

It was undertaken in a spirit of high responsibility and the audiences were treated throughout as completely adult. It was open-ended and escaped from the artificial pressures imposed by programme schedules. The questioning was done by men who were respected in their own right, instead of by professional interviewers, and there was no attempt to bully or hector those who took part. As a result of this, the temperature remained low, and in the absence of any sense of confrontation those who spoke did so moderately and intimately rather than rhetorically. There was no production gimmick, no music over captions, no studio audience to interrupt, and very few reaction shots. It was international – bringing together people from Britain and the Republic as well as Ulster – and those who were chosen were chosen because they were representative, and not just because they could be relied upon to argue well in a debate situation.

Perhaps the most important statement made on the programme came from Lord Devlin in summing up when he said: 'On questions of principle every citizen has a duty to form his own view.' This constitutional doctrine must necessarily carry with it the right of every citizen to have access to all the necessary information that will allow him to form his own views. Whether by design or not, the Devlin doctrine of the responsibility of a citizen conferred upon the media a duty that parliamentarians have hitherto claimed to be their special preserve. Indeed, the transcript of the BBC Ulster programme constitutes a State Paper of considerable importance, and the programme itself was certainly more influential than the debates that have occurred in the Parliaments at Westminster, Stormont or Dublin, all of which have necessarily been limited by their composition and the exclusion of the general public from the audience. The BBC programme reached millions of people.

Another recent example of the innovation in television coverage was the Harlech TV programme *My Brother's Keeper*, transmitted last month, which was actually made by the Transport and General Workers' Union in Bristol, with the help of highly qualified staff provided by Harlech, and in which the union presented itself without the intervention of any professional communicator as an intermediary.

Similarly some BBC local radio stations are beginning to work with local pressure groups to allow them to get their case across.

The Open University is perhaps the biggest single example of the transfer of substantial periods of broadcasting time to an outside body which uses the network purely as a publishing agent.

In conclusion, I submit the following criteria by which we might judge the media and determine the framework within which broadcasting should be contained, with a view to developing the necessary external and internal influences that ought to be brought to bear:

1. Is the content free from government control?
2. Do they provide regular access to allow individuals and groups to express specialist and minority views?
3. Do they sustain and reflect the rich and diverse inheritance that each community they serve draws from its past?
4. Is their coverage international, in the sense that uncensored material from other countries is regularly made available to their audiences?
5. Do they include serious and sustained education as part of their output?
6. Do they inform their communities about the future in time to allow public opinion to understand and influence their decisions before they are reached?
7. Is the majority of their revenue drawn from the service they provide, or does it come from advertising?
8. Do they operate any system of workers' self-management or industrial democracy?

9. Do those who work in them maintain any code of professional conduct?

10. Is there any independent body to whom they are accountable and which can investigate complaints made against them?

An ideal system would yield a positive answer to each of these questions.

Friday 9 August 1974

At 2 a.m. London time, Nixon gave his final broadcast as President. He made no real reference to Watergate and spoke as if he was a Prime Minister who had lost his parliamentary majority, full of the usual corny Nixon morality. An extraordinary broadcast. There was the fascination of seeing a great figure crushed; it was like a public execution. In the evening I listened to his emotional farewell to the staff of the White House, and President Ford's inaugural speech, full of Midwest homespun philosophy.

CHAPTER THREE

Lost Leader

In 1975 Tony Benn was fifty years old, one of the most energetic and talented members of the government, a potential Leader of the Labour Party, but whose wings had been clipped by Harold Wilson following the referendum in June on whether Britain should withdraw from the Common Market, or European Community. Tony had been a leading proponent of the referendum and, as soon as the result was known, he was moved from his job as Industry Secretary to Energy Secretary (marginally less powerful). In 1976 Wilson unexpectedly resigned as Prime Minister, and Tony threw his hat into the ring during the ensuing leadership election, which James Callaghan won. For the next five years he became something of a thorn in Callaghan's side as he embarked on a campaign of reform of the Labour Party, culminating in the deputy leadership contest in 1981 (which Denis Healey won by a fraction). Tony mused on the decision of the British people in the referendum to remain in Europe.

Saturday 1 March 1975

Today I got a letter, posted in London, written in purple felt pen to Mr Wedgewood (spelt wrongly) Benn, House of Commons. It read, 'You rotten traitor. Thank God you have only 7 more weeks.' I don't take much notice of death threats, I think because nobody has been murdered in the Palace of Westminster since Spencer Perceval, in 1806. But you never know, with George Brown's attack on me as an enemy of democracy, a good citizen might feel it his public duty to polish me off. I will just have to take reasonable precautions.

Sunday 2 March 1975

I had a telephone call from Allister Mackie of the Scottish Daily News. He told me that just before Bob Maxwell went to Moscow two days ago, he made a bid for the whole of the paper, insisting that in return for his £100,000 investment, he should be made Chairman and Chief Executive and the whole co-operative structure should be wound up, leaving him in charge. Allister said it was a terrible bombshell.

I said, 'Look, there are two points. First of all, remember that if Maxwell wants to take it over, it is the first real independent proof of viability because he wouldn't want to take over a dead duck. Secondly, call his bluff, don't change the prospectus because if you bring it back to ministers, they will kill it. So issue the prospectus as far as you can, as it is.'

He said he had a telephone call through to Maxwell in Moscow. An hour later he called me back saying he had made it clear to Maxwell that they were not prepared to accept his conditions and

Maxwell had backed down, so it looks as if they are safe. I was delighted.

————————◄○►————————

The European Community has set itself the objectives of developing a common foreign policy, a form of common nationality expressed through a common passport, a directly elected assembly and economic and monetary union which, taken together, would in effect make the United Kingdom into one province of a Western European state. Continued membership of the Community would therefore mean the end of Britain as a self-governing nation and of our democratically elected Parliament as the supreme law-making body of the United Kingdom.

The parliamentary democracy we have developed and established in Britain is based not upon the sovereignty of Parliament, but of the people, who, by exercising their vote, lend their sovereign powers to Members of Parliament to use on their behalf for the duration of a single parliament only – powers that must be returned intact to the electorate to whom they belong, to lend again to the Members of Parliament they elect in each subsequent general election. Five basic democratic rights derive from this relationship and each of them is fundamentally altered by Britain's membership of the European Community.

First, parliamentary democracy means that every man and woman over eighteen is entitled to vote to elect his or her Member of Parliament to service in the House of Commons, and the consent of the House of Commons is necessary before Parliament can pass any Act laying down new laws or imposing new taxation upon the people. British membership of the

Community subjects us all to laws and taxes which Members of Parliament do not enact. Instead such laws and taxes are enacted by authorities not directly elected and who cannot be dismissed through the ballot box.

Second, parliamentary democracy means that Members of Parliament who derive their powers directly from the British people can change any law and any tax by majority vote. British membership of the Community means that Community laws and taxes cannot be repealed or changed by the British Parliament, but only by the Community authorities, not directly elected by the British people.

Third, parliamentary democracy means that British courts and judges must uphold all laws passed by Parliament, and if Parliament changes any law, the courts must enforce the new law because it has been passed by Parliament, which has been directly elected by the people. British membership of the Community requires the British courts to uphold and enforce Community laws that have not been passed by Parliament and that Parliament cannot change or amend, even when such laws conflict with laws passed by Parliament, since the Community law overrides British law.

Fourth, parliamentary democracy means that all British governments, ministers and the civil servants under their control can only act within the laws of Britain and are accountable to Parliament for everything they do, and hence Parliament is accountable to the electors as a whole. British membership of the Community imposes upon British governments duties and constraints not deriving from the British Parliament and thus, in discharging those duties, ministers are not accountable to the British people who elect them.

Fifth, parliamentary democracy, because it entrenches the rights of the people to elect and dismiss Members of Parliament, also secures the continuing accountability of Members of Parliament to the electorate, obliging Members of Parliament to listen to the expression of the British people's views at all times – between, as well as during, general elections – and thus offers a continuing possibility of peaceful change through Parliament to meet the people's needs. British membership of the Community, by permanently transferring sovereign legislative and financial powers to Community authorities who are not directly elected by the British people, also permanently insulates those authorities from direct control by British electors, who cannot dismiss them and whose views therefore need carry no weight with them and whose grievances they cannot be compelled to remedy.

In short, the power of the electors of Britain through their direct representatives in Parliament, to make laws, levy taxes, change laws which the courts must uphold and control the conduct of public affairs, has been substantially ceded to the European Community, whose Council of Ministers and Commission are neither collectively elected nor collectively dismissed by the British people, nor even by the people of all the Community countries put together.

These five rights have protected us in Britain from the worst abuse of power by government, safeguarded us against the excesses of bureaucracy, defended our basic liberties, offered us the prospect of peaceful change, reduced the risk of civil strife, and bound us together by creating a national framework of consent for all the laws under which we were governed.

Depending on how the world develops, there could be a growing tendency to allow the Common Market to develop in a military or quasi-military direction. This would begin with small and innocent advances, such as international cooperation to deal with terrorism, and bringing the security forces together. Of course NATO and the Common Market are not entirely conterminous in their nature, but there could be circumstances in which the sinews of Common Market sovereignty begin to assert themselves in the military field, and we could find that the Commission had assumed the European responsibilities of NATO and was beginning to coordinate its military work. Once that happened, and it could easily happen over a generation or two, then there would be a military force also capable of enforcing the decisions of the European Court in support of the Treaty of Rome, if ever national opposition to the Court were to reach the point where it became insupportable. This is looking way ahead, but it would be foolish to leave out of account one possible direction of the European idea, in the minds of those who so strongly advocated our membership and who were most sincerely and deeply motivated by the idea of a European Federation in the immediate post-war period.

◄○►

Tuesday 16 March 1976

A day of such momentous news that it is difficult to know how to start.

After a meeting with Frances and Francis, I went to Cabinet at eleven. Harold said, 'Before we come to the business, I want to make a statement.' Then he read us an eight-page statement, in which he said that he had irrevocably decided that he was going to resign the premiership and would stay just long enough for the Labour Party to elect a new leader. People were stunned, but in a curious way, without emotion. Harold is not a man who arouses affection in most people. I sat there listening quite impassively and although other people were shocked and surprised, because nobody knew it was coming, there was still a remarkable sort of lack of reaction. But when he had finished speaking and thanked us all, Ted Short said, with visible sorrow – his eyes filled with tears and his face was red – 'I think this a deplorable event and I don't know what to say except to thank you.'

Bob Mellish said, 'I take it we'll proceed straight away to the election of a new leader.'

Jim Callaghan, who found it hard to conceal his excitement, said, 'Harold, we shall never be able to thank you for your services to the movement.'

Then Harold got up to go, because he had to see Len Murray and Cledwyn Hughes to tell them. He walked out of the Cabinet and that was it.

When he had gone, Shirley said, 'Don't you think we ought to formalise our thanks?' Barbara agreed, so the two of them began to draft something.

After a rather odd Cabinet, I left Downing Street at about one. By then there was a huge crowd of people, hundreds of television cameras. Over my ministerial lunch, we discussed why Harold had done it. Alex Eadie said the movement would be shaken and we had to protect against fears of a coalition. Then the question of who would stand for leader arose. Everyone had left except Frances, Francis and Joe, and Joe said, 'You must stand. You'll get a lot of votes.' Frances and Francis agreed.

I called Bryan Emmett in and I said, 'Now, look, you mustn't say to anybody that I'm standing because I haven't made up my mind yet, but I want the decks completely cleared of all engagements. Just tell Bernard Ingham that you don't know what I'm doing.'

Went over to the House and into the Chamber. I sat on the front bench and Harold came in at 3.15 for Prime Minister's Questions, and a question on the Royal Commission on the press provided an opportunity for everyone to pay tribute to Harold. Margaret Thatcher wished him well and suggested a general election. Jeremy Thorpe joked, most inappropriately, how nice it was to hear Harold was going on the back benches because it was such a comfort for a leader to have his predecessor beside him. Heath congratulated Harold on joining the fastest growing political 'party' in the House of Commons. Enoch Powell congratulated him for bringing peace to Ireland in contrast to the appalling policies of the previous government, which was an absolute hammer blow.

Thursday 20 January 1977

I got into the office at 8.30 this morning. Brian Sedgemore, whose appointment as my PPS was announced today, was there; we had a talk and went over a speech I am giving at a Tribune Group meeting tonight.

Cabinet. We came to Devolution and I raised one point – that in the provision for a referendum there should also be a referendum for electors in England. I said I forecast that we wouldn't get through a bill under which the English were not also allowed to vote.

At the end of the Cabinet I passed a note over to Jim. Yesterday he had sent round a minute to all senior ministers:

10 Downing Street

19 January 1977

BREVITY

The papers which I see – memoranda and reports addressed to me personally, as well as papers for Cabinet and its committees – are too long; and they seem recently to be getting longer.

We cannot afford inflation in words and paper, any more than in our currency. It is often harder work to be brief – but only for the writer. We shall all benefit as readers. Let us adopt again in our ministerial papers the habit of setting out in plain words, and in short paragraphs, the main points (detail in appendices, if need be) and the recommendations. The same discipline should apply to memoranda etc. addressed to the public bodies outside government and to the public. Please take any necessary action in your department to achieve this. Your Permanent Secretary should inform the Head of the Civil Service of what has been done and he will report to me.

L.J.C.

So in reply my note said:

PM

BREVITY

OK

A.W.B

19.1.77

and I attached to it an extract from Mao's collected works which began: 'Let us now analyse stereotyped Party writing and see where its evils lie.'

I feel my relations with Jim are improving. I think maybe he needs me on the industrial democracy front, and now that Sedgemore is appointed I feel more cheerful.

After lunch I had a meeting with Friends of the Earth, and we had a fascinating discussion about civil liberties and nuclear power. They put a lot of questions to me; I said I would get them answered and write to them.

Thursday 17 March 1977

Cabinet at ten. The first thing was that Jim said, 'I told the Cabinet I would buy a gift for the Queen and I asked her what she would like and she said she would like something she would use personally, something she really could use herself.' So Peter asked, 'Well, what is it?' He said, 'A silver coffee-pot.' Everyone laughed, because the one thing she must have a million of is silver coffee-pots. So anyway, Audrey Callaghan had gone out and found one and it was brought in and put on the table. It is Victorian and, since it will cost each member of the Cabinet £15, it is worth at least about £370.

I said, 'I assume that as it is a Cabinet coffee-pot it won't leak?' Jim said, 'You can say that to the Queen yourself.'

We went on to Carter, and Jim reported on his trip with David Owen to the United States. He said Jimmy Carter is a very fast reader, has an amazing capacity to absorb his briefs; he reads at something like 3,000 words a minute. 'About the same speed that Harold Wilson writes his books,' I said. Jim went on to say Carter was a great supporter of the Labour Party, and when Jim had told him, 'Well, we may save the country but lose the election', Carter had replied, 'Well, I hope you succeed with both.'

Tuesday 6 March 1979

Peter Jay came to the office for a talk. America is in serious economic difficulties and Carter, he said, was taking a terrible risk in trying to settle the Arab–Israeli conflict single-handedly – but that was the sort of man he was. Peter greatly admires Carter; he is a tough character and Peter responds to tough characters in the way that many intellectuals, such as Paul Johnson, gather round Mrs Thatcher.

We talked about when the general election might be …

To the House to vote in support of a bill by Maureen Colquhoun [Labour MP for Northampton] to abolish the status of the 'common prostitute', which was carried overwhelmingly. It was funny because the prostitutes' lobby had threatened to name any Member of Parliament known to have patronised a prostitute who voted against the bill. Those of us who voted for the bill were described as being in the 'red light lobby'.

◄○►

Speech to the Labour Party Conference, 1979

The Labour Party is a party of democratic, socialist reform. I know that for some people 'reform' is a term of abuse. That is not so. All our great successes have been the product of reform.

But if we are to take reform seriously then we must come to terms with the usual problem of the reformer; we have to run the economic system to protect our people, who are now locked into it while we change the system. And if you run it without seeking to change it, then you are locked in the decay of the system, but if you simply pass resolutions to change it without consulting those who are locked in the system that is decaying, then you become irrelevant to the people you seek to represent . . . We cannot content ourselves with speaking only to ourselves; we must raise these issues publicly and involve the community groups because we champion what they stand for. We must win the argument, broaden the base of membership, not only to win the election, but to generate the public support to carry the policies through.

<hr />

Monday 31 December 1979

Stansgate. In the evening Mother sat and talked; she is fascinating. She is eighty-three next year and first came to London in 1910 when Edward VII was on the throne. She knew Asquith, Lloyd George, Ramsay MacDonald and Arthur Henderson. She has a wide theological knowledge, and to hear her describing the various meanings of the immaculate conception, the physical ascension of Jesus and all that is so interesting.

Looking at the Thatcher government, it has begun implementing its reactionary policies with great vigour. Of course it is a unifying force for the labour movement at a time when our debates are inevitably internal and divisive. I don't know whether we will win the next election ... Certainly by the end of the Eighties there will be a great move forward towards reform, and I think we have to work towards that. It's going to be ten to fifteen years later than I thought in 1974.

<hr />

The month following this diary entry, in January 1980, Marxism Today published a comprehensive analysis by Tony Benn of Christianity as a revolutionary doctrine ('Revolutionary Christianity'). Although increasingly agnostic as he got older, Tony remained fascinated by the relationship between Christianity, radicalism and socialism.

When Jesus was asked by one of the Scribes, 'What commandment is the first of all?', St Mark's Gospel (chapter 12, verse 29) records his answer thus:

> 'The first is: Hear, O Israel: The Lord our God, the Lord is One: And thou shalt love the Lord thy God with all thy heart, and with all thy soul, and with all thy strength. And the second is this. Thou shalt love thy neighbour as thyself. There is none other Commandment greater than these.'

Any serving student of the teachings of the historical Jesus – and I lay claim to be such a student and no more – must take that passage as his starting point in the search for their revolutionary consequences.

Personal salvation seen as a revolutionary experience

Few would question the use of the word 'revolutionary' to describe the effect upon an individual of his or her conversion to the Christian faith with its sense of personal rebirth and the comforting certainty of eternal life.

Historically many churches appear to have been, and to remain, more concerned with the task of preaching personal salvation than with the social imperatives spelled out in Jesus's reply.

Generations of churchmen have formulated creeds and liturgies, have discussed the mystical aspects of theology and have worked within ecclesiastical hierarchies to interpret the word of God for the faithful, supported by various disciplines designed to secure their compliance.

The injunction to be good

It has also been true that ecclesiastical and temporal power have often been fused into a combined establishment to secure the submission of the people to the authoritarian demands of Church and State.

In such situations the social imperatives relating to our obligations to practise neighbourly love were shrunk into a vague and generalised injunction directed to the rich and powerful to express their love by being good and kind; and to the poor to return that love by being patient and submissive.

Both rich and poor, powerful and weak, were then reassured by the Church that in the world to come each would have their just reward and all suffering and injustice would be swept away for all eternity.

Neighbourly love as a revolutionary doctrine

Not surprisingly, this interpretation of the teachings of Jesus did not commend itself to the poor and the disinherited, who saw through this argument and rejected the role allocated to them in this world – of accepting injustice. Thus, outside the established churches, and in parallel with them, the practical commandment to practise true neighbourly love based upon an acceptance of our common humanity acquired an impetus of its own.

This radical interpretation of the teachings of Jesus spread wherever the Bible was available for study – and no doubt explains why the authorities were so anxious to keep it out of the hands of the laity. In this way the message reached and influenced a far wider audience – including those for whom social action was much more relevant and meaningful than the call to personal salvation.

H. G. Wells in his history of the world – himself an atheist – wrote this about the revolutionary nature of Jesus's teachings:

> In view of what he plainly said, is it any wonder that all who were rich and prosperous felt a horror of strange things, a swimming of their world at his teaching? He was dragging out all the little private reservations they had made from social service into the light of a universal religious life. He was like some terrible moral huntsman digging mankind out of the snug burrows in which they had lived hitherto. In the white blaze of this kingdom of his there was to be no property, no privilege, no pride and precedence; no motive indeed and no reward but love. Is it any wonder that men were dazzled and blinded and cried out against him? Even his disciples cried out when he would not spare them the light. Is it any wonder that the priests realised that between this man and themselves there was no choice but that he or priest-craft should perish? Is it any wonder that the Roman soldiers, confronted and amazed by something soaring over their comprehension and threatening all their disciplines, should take refuge in wild laughter and crown him with thorns and robe him in purple and make a mock Caesar out of him? For to take him seriously was to enter upon a strange and alarming life, to abandon habits, to control instincts and impulses, to essay an incredible happiness.

The secularisation of the Christian ethic

This radical interpretation of the message of brotherhood and its clear anti-establishment agitation has surfaced time and again throughout our history. Wycliffe and the Lollards were engaged in it. So was the Reverend John Ball, whose support for the Peasants' Revolt cost him his life in 1381.

The belief in the 'priesthood of all believers', which lies at the root of Congregationalism, and the Quakers' 'inner light' were – and remain – profoundly revolutionary in their impact upon the hierarchies of the Church itself. Nor was this revolutionary agitation confined to the Church.

The 'divine right of kings' asserted by King Charles I as a defence of his powers was overthrown, along with the King himself, and in the ensuing revolution a furious debate began about the legitimacy of the organs of both Church and State power.

The Levellers expressed their political philosophy in Christian terms:

> The relation of Master and Servant has no ground in the New Testament; in Christ there is neither bond nor free. Ranks such as those of the peerage and gentry are 'ethnical and heathenish distinctions'. There is no ground in nature or Scripture why one man should have £1000 per annum, another not £1. The common people have been kept under blindness and ignorance, and have remained servants and slaves to the nobility and gentry. But God have now opened their eyes and discovered unto them their Christian liberty.

Gerrard Winstanley – the true Leveller, or Digger – went further and defined the Creator not as God but as 'Reason', and on that basis rejected the historical justification for the doctrine that 'one branch of mankind should rule over another':

> In the beginning of Time, the great Creator, Reason, made the Earth to be a Common Treasury, to preserve Beasts, Birds,

Fishes and Man, the lord that was to govern this Creation; for Man had Domination given to him, over the Beasts, Birds and Fishes, but not one word was spoken in the beginning, that one branch of mankind should rule over another.

And the reason is this, every single man, Male and Female, is a perfect Creature of himself; and the same Spirit that made the Globe dwells in man to govern the Globe; so that the flesh of man being subject to Reason, his Maker, hath him to be his Teacher and Ruler within himself, therefore needs not run abroad after any Teacher and Ruler without him, for he needs not that any man should teach him, for the same Anoynting that ruled in the Son of Man, teacheth him all things.

But since humane flesh (that king of Beasts) began to delight himself in the objects of the Creation, more than in the Spirit Reason and Righteousness . . . covetousness, did set up one man to teach and rule over another, and thereby the Spirit was killed, and man was brought into bondage and became a greater Slave to such of his own kind, than the Beasts of the field were to him.

The bridge between Christianity and humanism

In this way a bridge was constructed that carried the message of brotherhood and sisterhood from Christianity to secular humanism, a bridge that carried the ethics across but left the creeds behind. Across this bridge there is now a growing two-way traffic of people and ideas. Christians involved in political action cross it one way. Humanists can cross it to go back to the teachings of Jesus and study them.

In a theological sense there is a great divide between the Christians on one side and the humanists on the other.

But it is impossible to escape the conclusion that over that bridge revolutionary ideas deriving from the Bible and the Carpenter of Nazareth have spread to influence hundreds of millions of people for whom the need for neighbourly love within a common humanity is immediately apparent in a way that the mysticism, liturgies and needs may appear to be less relevant.

The political effect of the preaching of brotherhood

It has also been along this route that many Christian values have travelled until they became embedded in our society as 'sacred' human rights that ought to be upheld in our political life. Thus did the American colonists proclaim it in their Declaration of Independence in 1776:

> We hold these Truths to be self-evident, that all Men are created equal, that they are endowed by their Creator with certain inalienable Rights, that among these are Life, Liberty and the Pursuit of Happiness. That to secure these Rights, Governments are instituted among Men deriving their just Powers from the Consent of the Governed.

There are many other examples to cite.

The environmental movement

Environmentalists and ecologists assert that we are all stewards of the earth, on behalf of our brothers and sisters and our children and grandchildren, for whose right to live free from pollution we are morally responsible and politically accountable. They are revolutionaries too, in their hostility to exploitation of the planet and its people by feudalism, capitalism or any temporal authority.

The assertion of conscience above the law

The deeply held conviction that conscience is above the law – because conscience is God-given and laws are made by men and women – is also highly revolutionary, yet the struggles to assert it, and those who died to secure it, are the true founders of our civil liberties – including the right to worship in our own way and to hold dissenting political views.

Democracy as a moral issue

Perhaps the greatest inheritance that this country has derived from the teachings of Jesus has been the heritage of democracy itself – with all the political ideas that are associated with it.

If we are our 'brother's and our sister's keeper', then an 'injury to one is an injury to all' and from that derive most of our contemporary ideas about solidarity and the moral responsibilities of trade unions.

The right of each man or woman to vote in elections also stems from their right to be treated as fully human and equal in the sight of God.

So too does the pressure for social justice and greater equality, which the ballot box allows the electors to exercise through their vote. So too does the internationalism which is a part and parcel of socialism that has never accepted any divine authority for nationalism at the expense of others. All this was beautifully summed up in the words of the Great Charter issued by the Chartists in 1842:

The great Political Truths which have been agitated during the last half-century have at length aroused the degraded and insulted White Slaves of England to a sense of their duty to themselves, their children and their country. Tens of thousands have flung down their implements of labour. Your taskmasters tremble at your energy, and expecting masses eagerly watch this great crisis of our cause. Labour must no longer be the common prey of masters and rulers. Intelligence has beamed upon the mind of the bondsman, and he has been convinced that all wealth, comfort and produce, everything valuable, useful, and elegant, have sprung from the palm of his hand; he feels that his cottage is empty, his back thinly clad, his children breadless, himself hopeless, his mind harassed, and his body punished, that undue riches, luxury and gorgeous plenty might be heaped in the palaces of the taskmasters, and flooded into the granaries of the oppressor. Nature, God, and Reason have condemned this inequality, and in the thunder of a people's voice it must perish for ever.

These are some of the reasons why so many democratic socialists in this country look back to the teachings of Jesus as a major and continuing source of political inspiration over centuries of thought and effort. For many Christians such openly secular interpretations of the teachings of Jesus may seem to separate those who hold them completely from the creeds of Christian faith. It is argued that without the acceptance of a personal God whose Fatherhood is ever-present, the brotherhood and sisterhood of men and women loses its meaning and the teachings of Christ degenerate into mere ethics.

In order to consider that argument it is necessary to look back into history and consider how, in the past, Christianity came to terms with the then equally threatening challenge of the natural sciences.

How Christianity adjusted to the natural sciences

In past centuries the faith of a Christian would have been defined in such a way as to require him or her to deny the validity of all scientific enquiry into the nature of the universe or the origins of man if they conflicted with the Book of Genesis. Galileo fell foul of the Church.

Darwin was denounced for his *Origins of Species* and so were all those who challenged the most literal interpretation of the words of the Old Testament. Indeed, Darwin was forced to admit in 1870: 'My theology is a simple muddle. I cannot look upon the universe as the result of blind chance. Yet I can see no evidence of beneficent design, or indeed of design of any kind in the details.'

Darwin became an agnostic, was buried in Westminster Abbey, and today few Christians would find difficulty in reconciling his theories of evolution with their Christian faith.

Scientists who study the working of Nature are now accepted as they are, without being seen as heretics. Today Christian fundamentalism remains as a respected position to occupy, and since fundamentalists no longer have the political power to persecute science, science has no interest in discrediting fundamentalism.

They coexist in peace. That struggle is over. It was a struggle against the Church and not against the teachings of Jesus.

The challenge of socialism and Marxism to the Church

But how should Christians respond to the challenge of completely secular socialism and Marxism, which for over a century have consciously disconnected their view of brotherhood and sisterhood from the Church and its creeds and mysteries? Such socialists believe that the continuing denial of our common humanity does not derive solely, or even primarily, from the sinful conduct of

97

individuals, but is institutionalised in the structures of economic, industrial and political power which Christian churches may support, sustain and even bless, whilst turning a blind eye to the injustices that continue unchecked.

Socialists argue that neighbourly love must be sought in this world and not postponed until the next one. They do not believe that priestly injunctions restricted to matters of personal conduct – 'Be good' or Be kind' – are any substitute whatsoever for the fundamental reforms that require collective political action.

The socialist interpretation of the parable of the Good Samaritan would cast many Churches and churchmen in the role of the priest and the Levite who passed by on the other side; and would identify the socialist position with that of the Good Samaritan, who was less concerned with the personal salvation of the traveller who was stripped and beaten than with his immediate need for medical treatment, accommodation and food in this world here and now.

Unless Christians can respond institutionally and politically to that socialist challenge, their faith can become an escape from reality and, indeed, an escape from the challenge posed by Jesus himself.

In a world characterised by brutal repression and exploitation under regimes of all kinds, Christian escapism is no more acceptable than it was on the road to Jericho.

The Christian response considered

How should Christians answer this challenge? It is just not good enough to declare a holy war on socialism and Marxism, on the grounds that they are atheistical. That is how, historically, the Catholics treated the Protestants, and the Protestants treated the Catholics – burning each other at the stake. Yet that is the approach advocated by many Christian anti-communist crusaders, which lies behind the harassment of Marxists in many Western capitalist countries, including Britain; and in all countries living under anti-communist military dictatorships.

But before adopting such a position it is necessary to consider other interpretations of the true meaning of Marxism.

Dr Nathaniel Micklem had this to say in his book *A Religion of Agnostics:* 'Though he disguised his moral indignation under cover of scientific terminology, was it in response to the call of a higher and more lasting justice that Karl Marx repudiated the "bourgeois" inequality of his day?'

This view was echoed by Ivan Sviták in his speech at Charles University during the Prague Spring on 3 May 1968:

Marx was not, and is not, and never will be, the inventor and theoretician of totalitarian dictatorship that he appears today, when the original meaning of his work – true humanism – has been given a thoroughly Byzantine and Asian twist. Marx strove for a wider humanism than that of the bourgeois democracies that he knew, and for wider civil rights, not for the setting-up of the dictatorship of one class and one political party. What is today thought to be the Marxist theory of the State and the Marxist social science imply an ideological forgery, a false contemporary conception, as wrong as the idea that the orbits of heavenly bodies are circular.

Milan Machovec, in his book *A Marxist Looks at Jesus*, carried this argument a stage further forward in assessing the Marxist view of Jesus:

You can corrupt the heritage, overlay what is best in it, or push it into the background, but those who seek it out tomorrow will find life and new hope beneath the layers of dirt and the petrified outlines – simply because they are attuned to it. Thus in Christianity the dogmatised image of Jesus Christ has never been able thoroughly to banish the image of the man, Jesus of Nazareth.

That view of the relationship between the teachings of Jesus and the writings of Marx merits very serious consideration. If that view prevails – as I believe it may – a century from now the writings of Marx may be seen as no more threatening to the teachings of Jesus than the writings of Darwin are now thought to be today.

The case against an institutional concordat

I am not urging a political concordat between the hierarchies of the Vatican, the Kremlin and Lambeth Palace – which, if they merged, all their historical experience of centralised organisation and bureaucracy could pose – it might be argued – the greatest threat to freedom of conscience the world has ever seen.

The urgent need for a broader oecumenical movement

But I am saying that as the oecumenical movement gathers momentum – and if it remains a mosaic and does not become a monolith – it should extend the range of its dialogue to embrace socialists and Marxists as well as Catholics, Protestants, Jews, Buddhists and Muslims. And there is one compelling reason why it must.

The technology of destruction at the disposal of mankind in modern weapons, and the rocketry to deliver them, must now require us all to open our hearts and minds to the inescapable need for neighbourly love on a global scale and then build the social, political and economic institutions that can express it, bringing together those who now marshal themselves under different banners of religious and political faith.

A holy war with atom bombs could end the human family for ever.

A personal view

I say all this as a socialist whose political commitment owes much more to the teachings of Jesus – without the mysteries within which they are presented – than to the writings of Marx, whose analysis seems to lack an understanding of the deeper needs of humanity.

But untold numbers of people all over the world – and I am one of them – are now claiming the right to study all the sources of insight which they find meaningful, and reach their own personal conclusions about their significance, free from the threat of excommunication for failing to satisfy the tenets of faith laid down by any church or any party.

In that sense, too, the teachings of Jesus can be seen as truly revolutionary and to have spread its influence far beyond the bounds of Christendom.

————◄◦►————

Sunday 7 December 1980

Woke at six and turned on the television and for one hour I listened to a man called Pat Robertson, who runs a right-wing born-again Christian evangelical movement. It was such a hair-raising programme that it undid all the optimism that I had begun to feel when I came to the conference. This guy Pat Robertson, who looked like a business executive of about forty-five with one of those slow, charming American smiles, was standing there with a big tall black man beside him, his sidekick, and he talked continuously about the Reagan administration, about the defeat of the liberals, about Reagan's commitment to the evangelical movement. He had a blackboard showing what in the nineteenth century 'liberal' meant. He then wiped that from the blackboard and said that today the liberals are Marxists, Fascists, leftists and socialists.

Then he showed an extract of Reagan saying, 'We want to keep big government out of our homes, and out of our schools, and out of our family life.' He went on and on for an hour like this. At the end, he said, 'Let us pray', and, his face contorted with fake piety, pleaded with Jesus to protect America, 'our country'.

I couldn't switch it off. It was so frightening, the feeling that we are now entering a holy war between that type of reactionary Christianity and communism. It is a thoroughly wicked and evil interpretation of Christianity.

<hr />

By 1981 the Conservatives were back in government under Margaret Thatcher, and Tony Benn was preparing to launch a campaign for the deputy leadership of the Labour Party. At the same time he became very ill with a disease, Guillain-Barré syndrome, from which he recovered, but lost some mobility permanently. In March of that year he took on afresh the question of Europe, in the context of the two powers on either side – America and the Soviet Union.

European Unity: A New Perspective

I want to examine Europe, divided between East and West, and then look much further ahead to new possibilities of cooperation that may exist for the future of our continent in the Nineties and beyond. In brief, can we unite the whole of Europe in the next generation?

If Europe is to survive, and humanity is to be spared a nuclear holocaust, we *must* attempt that task.

There must be fresh thinking, and a new agenda.

The present division is symbolised by the Berlin Wall: on the one side the communist countries under the influence of Moscow; on the other the West under the umbrella of America.

The two alliances, NATO and the Warsaw Pact, are both heavily armed with nuclear weapons, strategic, theatre and tactical – numbering between 10,000 and 15,000 missiles in position.

Massive ground, air and naval forces are also deployed on both sides.

Army limitation talks, especially on the Strategic Arms Limitation Treaty, are deadlocked and arms expenditure is now planned to rise still further.

The military establishments controlling these forces and this technology are funded on a large scale, command huge industrial resources, and are getting more and more powerful inside each nation that sustains them and, as a result, are getting harder and harder to control politically.

Meanwhile, in the background the two superpowers have problems of their own, which greatly influence their respective approaches to Europe.

Mr Brezhnev is faced with a major revolt against Soviet domination in Poland, where working people are seeking greater democracy in their lives, and has sent troops into Afghanistan, in an attempt to secure the southern flank against what he perceives to be infiltration. Who knows what other revolts lie under the surface in and around the USSR?

President Reagan is faced with a major revolt against American dominance in El Salvador, and is demanding the use of Western European troops in a NATO Rapid Deployment Force, to safeguard Western interests worldwide. Who knows what other revolts against US power lie under the surface in and around the USA?

Both the superpowers have their own interests in Europe, but the division of our continent is not quite as sharp and clear as might be supposed.

Yugoslavia and Albania, each under a communist government, stand apart from their neighbours in COMECON [Soviet-led Council for Mutual Economic Assistance].

And the West is not monolithic, either, for, even allowing for further enlargement to include Spain and Portugal, the EEC does not include Sweden, Norway, Finland, Austria or Switzerland.

The complex pattern of European systems is a product of the past: the First World War, the Russian Revolution, the growth of Fascism, the Second World War and the subsequent tension which has persisted since.

The 1914–18 conflict derived from a clash of imperial interests. It inflicted serious damage on all the participants, and laid the foundation for much of what has happened since.

In 1920 the United States went into isolation, and the European economies, severely damaged by war, were thrown into slump and mass unemployment, which first brought Mussolini to power in Italy; then Hitler to power in Germany, Franco in Spain, Salazar in Portugal, and brought almost the whole of Europe under the control of the Nazis, from 1940 to 1945. The world war then brought the US back into Europe. It also encouraged great hopes for a new Europe amongst that generation – hopes which have never yet been realised.

The Russian Revolution has dominated the century as the French Revolution did in its time. It was a turning point in world history, and from then until now it has been the objective of various Western leaders to contain Soviet power or to overturn the regime itself.

A British Expeditionary Force was sent to support the White Armies at Archangel in 1919.

Twenty-two years later the German armies launched their blitzkrieg against the USSR, laying waste their territory and killing twenty-five million Russians.

And as late as 17 April 1948 the American Ambassador in London, in a despatch to the US Secretary of State, reported on his talks with Winston Churchill in these words: 'He' – that is, Churchill – 'believes that now is the time, promptly, to tell the Soviets that if they do not retire from Berlin and abandon Eastern Germany, withdrawing to the Polish frontier, we will raze their cities.'

It is necessary to remind ourselves of all these events in order to explain the developments of the last thirty years.

For just as the West built up its defences under the American umbrella which gave birth to NATO; and built up its economies under the Marshall Plan and created the EEC; the Russians look to their defence system in terms of a *cordon sanitaire* of communist states on their western border – including Eastern Germany – and established the Warsaw Pact to protect themselves from a fourth attack from the West.

The dominant factor in European politics today remains fear of attack by both East and West from each other.

In the West the Soviet control of East Germany, Czechoslovakia, Poland, Hungary, Bulgaria and Rumania is widely interpreted as clear evidence of Soviet intentions to expand its control over the whole of Europe, and the military arsenals of the Warsaw Pact, with their heavy preponderance of ground troops, add to those fears.

In Moscow the situation must look very different.

Given Russia's past experience, the hostility of China, and the immense technical, industrial and economic superiority of the USA, the Kremlin calculates the balance of military forces on a different basis, which must look a great deal less favourable to them.

But the insecurity in America and Russia is not limited to their assessment of the external military threat as each sees it.

For the Kremlin fears that the regimes in the Warsaw Pact countries would be unlikely to survive any genuine test of public opinion in a free election.

And even at home, sixty-four years after the October Revolution, the repression of political opposition indicates that their system is still too vulnerable to survive the rigours of too much free debate.

State communism is still not willing to put itself to the proof of public support, which we would accept as democratic.

Nor is America without its own anxieties.

The election of President Reagan suggests that millions of Americans sense and resent the evident decline of American power in the world – even close to home, as in Latin America – and feel the need to assert themselves militarily to stop the rot. Will it lead to a US military adventure against Cuba, just as a similar post-imperial crisis of self-confidence tempted Sir Anthony Eden into his attack on Egypt in 1956?

The US is also now in the grip of a massive economic recession, which poses acute internal problems and is not the best possible advertisement for the virtues of capitalism. This slump is also affecting Western Europe.

Europe is therefore now caught up in the middle of this impasse between the superpowers, both of which show signs of being paralysed by their own deep sense of insecurity.

But unless Europeans are content to remain pawns in a superpower chess game, we must seek to make our own judgements of what is happening, and why.

It is necessary for us first to consider whether we really believe the warnings that issue from Washington about Moscow's intentions; or from Moscow about Washington's plans.

My judgement is that both the Pentagon and the Kremlin are mistaken if they believe that the other is seriously planning for world domination.

Each appears to be behaving exactly as Great Powers have always behaved – determined to safeguard their own homeland and vital interests; and seeking to extend their influence and interests and their ideology as far as they have the power to do so.

That certainly was Britain's posture during the heyday of the Victorian Empire, and it even led Britain into an invasion of Afghanistan in the nineteenth century.

But it is not credible to believe, in the age of nuclear weapons, that either superpower is preparing for expansion by war. And if either were to attempt it, by non-nuclear means, their plans would encounter such violent hostility worldwide and in the countries they occupied that they could not hope to succeed.

Some judgement of the intentions of the superpowers has to be made, if Europe is to look to its own future in its own right.

For as soon as we have cleared our own minds we can plan accordingly.

For those who believe that it is only a matter of time before the Red Army marches on the West, preceded by a bombardment from SS20 missiles, then mass mobilisation together with a crash programme of nuclear rearmament and civil-defence measures is the proper course.

And if Russia really expects a direct attack on her security system she will activate her troops in Poland, establish military regimes in every

Warsaw Pact country, and expand her nuclear-weapons programme.

The reality is, of course, very different.

Despite the renewal of the Cold War and the escalation of the arms race, the real Europe does not behave as if it believed in the inevitability of war.

Nor does the pattern of life in Europe, as it is, correspond at all with the rigid division between East and West which the superpower strategists seek to impose upon it in their speeches and writings.

This becomes clear as soon as any of the simple litmus-paper tests are applied to the real world.

First, is it true that the conflict can be clarified in terms of ideology? Are we facing a holy war between 'Christian capitalism and atheistic communism'?

Those who argue that case would have a difficult task to sustain it. There is too much evidence which points the other way.

Yugoslavia is a Marxist state receiving political support from the West.

In Poland the Church and the Communist Party have avoided confrontation, by accepting coexistence.

Similarly, in the West, Marx has always been accepted as a towering socialist intellectual by most democratic socialist parties.

Many dissidents in Eastern Europe have denounced Stalinism on the grounds that it is a vicious distortion of the teachings of Marx.

In Western Europe the Communist Parties are no longer the monolithic blocs they were once thought to be. In Italy and Spain great changes have been made in organisational terms to allow more broad-based discussion, accepting political pluralism and rejecting the doctrine of the dictatorship of the proletariat. This is similar to the demands made in Gdansk last year, in the Prague Spring of 1968; and in Budapest in 1956.

No black-and-white division based on ideology stands up to examination.

It would be truer to say that there is a growing demand for democracy in the communist states, and for socialism in the states which accept parliamentary democracy.

The second untruth is that the Iron Curtain is impenetrable.

Look at the Ostpolitik of the Federal Republic of Germany and the human contacts that have been allowed. Look at the special relationship between Austria and Hungary that benefits both countries. These contacts are also developing in the Balkans.

Consider the pattern of trade between East and West. In 1978 Western Europe as a whole exported US $18 billion-worth of goods to Eastern Europe and imported US $20 billion-worth in return. And in 1980, in spite of the increase in international tension, intra-German trade remained high and profitable.

Even in energy, which is of vital importance to the world economy, Soviet gas exports and Polish coal exports to the West, though temporarily reduced, are a part of the economy of the real Europe and play an important role in its mutual prosperity. Europe needs an energy plan worked out, in detail, between East and West.

And, following the Helsinki Accords, there is growing contact in cultural matters and exchanges of visits and delegations, although they could be increased still further. The BBC World Service plays an important part in the process.

Many Western countries have technological agreements with the USSR and Eastern Europe. France pioneered them, then Germany, and I signed many of them myself as the British Minister of Technology in the 1960s. Later, my own direct experience as Secretary of State with responsibility for nuclear matters taught me that there is even a close accord on the issue of proliferation of nuclear weapons, to which the Soviet Union is as strongly opposed as is the USA.

Even the denial of human rights is by no means confined to the communist countries, as memories of Franco's Spain, Salazar's Portugal and today's Third World dictatorships backed by the West remind us.

Europe is living together, and working together, and changing its prospects by doing so. The restoration of democracy in Portugal and Spain is very significant in this context.

This is the reality to which we must turn our eyes.

Europe is a huge continent.

Excluding the USSR, the traditional Europe consists of twenty-nine countries; ten in the EEC; eleven outside the EEC; and eight in COMECON.

Its total area is nearly six million square kilometres and its total population is over 500 million.

Together its national income added up in 1978 to US $27,700 billion.

To speak of the continent as a whole will be so strange to the ears of many people, and to consider plans for its future, in cooperation, may seem visionary at this moment.

But despite all that has happened, there is a strong common interest on which to build.

The surest starting point must be the demonstrable desire of all the people of Europe for the achievement of certain minimum necessities of life itself.

The people of Poland, like the people of Portugal; or the inhabitants of the two Germanies; or of Britain and Czechoslovakia – must necessarily hope and pray for peace for themselves and their families.

Everyone wants work and good housing, healthcare and adequate schooling, opportunities for the young, dignity in retirement, and a fair distribution of wealth.

And the majority would like to enjoy full human rights and political and trade-union freedom so that they can organise and express themselves openly and without fear of victimisation.

Women want equality, and ethnic and cultural minorities want safeguards. Everybody would prefer to live in circumstances which allow them a real say over those who govern them. And the demand for regional self-determination is to be found in many countries.

Unfortunately nowhere in Europe today are *all* these rights achieved or aspirations met.

But for anyone who seeks to uphold these rights it is clear that there is a stronger common interest amongst common people in detente and disarmament than in tension and the arms race.

If that is all true – and it is so obvious as to be beyond argument – we have to turn our minds to those policies which might move us towards their realisation.

Any serious attempt to identify such policies must begin with the problems of security. Every government, of whatever political complexion, always makes security its first priority. That was the foundation upon which both the League of Nations and the United Nations based their Charters.

We must then ask ourselves how that security is to be achieved, and whether the balance of nuclear terror satisfies that requirement.

I cite only one witness on this issue: Lord Mountbatten, a Supreme Commander of World War II, who, just before his death, delivered a remarkable lecture on this very subject. Speaking at the Stockholm International Peace Research Institute on 11 May 1979, Mountbatten said:

> As a military man who has given half a century of
>   military service, I say in all sincerity that the nuclear arms

race has no military purpose. Wars cannot be fought with nuclear weapons. Their existence only adds to our perils because of the illusions which they have generated.

There are powerful voices around the world who still give credence to the old Roman precept – 'If you desire peace, prepare for war.' This is absolute nuclear nonsense, and I repeat – it is a disastrous misconception to believe that by increasing the total uncertainty one increases one's own certainty.

A growing number of Europe's half-billion population would share that judgement, and I am one of them.

How can we reverse the drift to nuclear war?

The most hopeful initiative that has emerged in Europe has been the growing demand for European Nuclear Disarmament to make our whole continent a nuclear-free zone.

It has been canvassed by ministers over the years in both East and West, in speeches by Poles, Czechs and East Germans. The Irish Government touched on it in 1959 and the Swedes and Finns have also promoted it.

Last year the European Nuclear Disarmament Movement began to gather momentum in West Europe, including Britain, and an appeal for support was launched in several capitals, and it has met with an encouraging response.

This groundswell of opinion is growing as the arms race threatens to grow.

It would be a mistake to present this argument in terms of pacifism.

For many who are not pacifists now see nuclear weapons as a recipe for mass destruction, and not as a defence policy at all. Others – like the British Labour Party – have decided to oppose all military strategies based upon the threat or use of nuclear weapons, and favour a non-nuclear defence policy, rejecting Trident, and Cruise missiles, and the deployment of the Neutron bomb. We want a defence policy that would defend our homeland and its people, not one which threatens to obliterate it.

Here is a campaign which really does offer a future with some hope, instead of the acceptance of fear as the main driving force for security.

Moreover, experience since 1945 strongly suggests – as Vietnam and Algeria established, and Afghanistan and Poland may prove yet again – that a determined people is the best guarantee against permanent domination from outside. Decisions about peace and war cannot be subcontracted to a man in a bomb-proof shelter with control over a nuclear button.

The Swedes and the Swiss have certainly founded their defence strategy upon 'dissuasion' rather than 'deterrence' and it makes a lot more sense to examine that option carefully. Both have a large citizen army that can be mobilised very quickly and would inflict immense casualties on any invader, without nuclear weapons or creating a military elite that could organise a domestic coup.

But security is not entirely an external problem.

Internal security must necessarily rest in the end upon a foundation of popular consent.

For example, the French Revolution with its battle cry 'Liberty, Equality and Fraternity', overthrew the *ancien régime* of the Bourbons, which did not enjoy that consent.

The appeal for popular support for socialism was defined in 1848 in these words: 'The free development of each is the condition for the free development of all.'

And in El Salvador last July the present Pope said: 'Any society which does not wish to be destroyed from within must establish a just social order.'

These beliefs, and the commitment to achieve them, inspired the British trade unions, when they demanded the vote for the working class in Britain more than a hundred years ago, just as the Polish trade unions have raised the same cry today. And it is the same voices from the Third World which are now demanding social justice and a new world economic order through the UN.

The achievement of domestic justice and domestic security is a great deal easier when no external threat can be used as an excuse for internal repression.

That too points to the desirability of détente, rather than a nuclear arms race.

It also points to the importance of stimulating trade and commerce between East and West, and seeking to interlock the economies of the two blocs so tightly that interdependence makes conflict increasingly difficult, and ultimately impossible.

In this context we have to decide whether it is in our interests in the West for the economy of Eastern Europe to fail or to succeed.

State communism and its international system must be transformed from the inside, and it is in our interests to allow that to happen. These internal reforms are much more likely to succeed if they can take place within a framework of growing European cooperation and détente, and without raising the spectre of a security threat for the Russians, which their military leaders might then use as an excuse for intervention.

But pressure for internal reform is not confined to Eastern Europe.

The Western economies are stagnating, with high and chronic unemployment and cut-backs in essential services.

There are today eight and a half million unemployed in the EEC;

and, allowing for two dependants in every household, this means that nearly twenty-five million people in the Common Market are now living in homes where the breadwinner is out of work and the family income is dependent upon social benefits, the real value of which may be eroded by inflation.

The challenge to this generation is how to return to full employment without rearmament and war.

It is against this background that the whole philosophy of the Treaty of Rome, which entrenches and sanctifies market forces, will now be judged.

The most telling critique of that Treaty which is now emerging is not based upon national interests, but upon its inherent defects and the undemocratic nature of the Commission itself, which operate against the true interests of the peoples in all member states.

As the Community changes by enlargement – or withdrawal – the pressure for a much looser and wider association of fully self-governing states in Europe is likely to be canvassed and could transform the whole nature of European co-operation in the West.

It is not too soon to begin thinking about Europe in the twenty-first century, which lies less than nineteen years ahead.

Our vision must be of peace, jobs and freedom, achieved between fully self-governing states within a security system ultimately replacing both the Warsaw Pact and NATO. We must envisage a multi-polar world well disposed to America and Russia, but under the control of neither. Europe must play a full part in the UN to realise the aims of its Charter, and respect the demands for self-determination and independence in Third World countries, with whom we must establish a constructive dialogue.

It is a vision for our children and our children's children, and in that spirit I commend it for your consideration.

I offer you a text for tomorrow's Europe. It comes from Mahatma Gandhi, whose advocacy of non-violence makes him a fitting prophet for today:

> I do not want my house to be walled in on all sides nor my
> windows to be shut.
>   I want the culture of all lands to blow about my house,
> as freely as possible, but I refuse to be blown off my feet by
> any of them.

CHAPTER FOUR

Caged

After the election of the Conservatives in 1979, Tony Benn was never again to serve in a Labour government. The period of self-destructive introspection that began in the Labour Party in the 1970s resulted in the emergence of a new party, the Social Democratic Party (of Roy Jenkins, Shirley Williams, David Owen and William Rodgers), in 1981 and the eventual merger of the SDP with the Liberal Party in 1988. After Tony lost Bristol South East in the post-Falklands 1983 general election, his political career appeared to be over, until he was given a new lease of life as MP for Chesterfield, at the heart of the Derbyshire mining community.

With the rapid demise of his support base in the 1980s, Tony was somewhat beyond the pale of the Parliamentary Labour Party; he turned to journalism, writing a number of analytical essays on socialism for Marxism Today, *and concentrated his energies on extra-parliamentary action, for example in support of the miners during the 1984–5 national strike, of the News International workers at Wapping, East London, in their protracted dispute with Rupert Murdoch, and against the 'Poll*

Tax'. He used the House of Commons to argue against the Conservative policies that aimed to reverse the social and economic status quo – policies that included the wide-scale privatisation of industries which had been in public ownership after the war.

In 1986 Tony was approached by the publisher Hutchinson to publish the diaries that he had kept on and off since the 1940s, and systematically since 1964; and he employed me, first as transcriber and subsequently as editor, to work on the many millions of words he had amassed. The next year Out of the Wilderness *was born, the first volume in a project that gave him a new focus and a new audience in the ensuing twenty-five years.*

Tuesday 2 March 1982

Norman Atkinson told me that Rupert Murdoch had had lunch with Mrs Thatcher no less than three times last week. He had heard that from Ian Gow, Mrs Thatcher's PPS, and he had the impression that the Tories were panic-stricken that *The Times* might come out for the SDP. So they were offering Murdoch all possible help in return for support for the Tory Party.

Monday 22 March 1982

To London Airport to get the flight to Glasgow, and who should I see at the airport but David and Debbie Owen going to Hillhead to campaign in the by-election for Roy Jenkins, who is standing as the SDP–Liberal Alliance candidate. Then George Brown came in and headed for the bar. So sitting in the airport were three people who had been Cabinet ministers together at different times, and two of them had defected and were going to speak for Roy

Jenkins. Brown and Jenkins – two former Deputy Leaders of the Labour Party.

I was met at Glasgow and taken to the Hillhead Labour Party committee rooms, where I had a cup of tea and a bun. Then I was taken into a little room in an old Co-op funeral parlour where the candidate, David Wiseman, and others were gathered – a panelled room where no doubt grieving Glaswegians were handed the bill for burying their relatives. Helen Liddell, the secretary of the Scottish Council of the Labour Party, said they were frightened about my coming – Helen is very right-wing. They kept bringing up 'extremism' in the Party and said, 'Your Marx Memorial Lecture didn't help.'

I went to the meeting attended by 1,500–2,000 people. The SDP had put out a little red-baiting, McCarthyite-type leaflet referring to my lecture.

<hr>

'Democracy and Marxism' was a major analysis of the influence of Karl Marx on the world. It was a stout defence of the man 'sometimes regarded as an Old Testament prophet' but it failed to anticipate the coming implosion of the Soviet-led communist world.

The intellectual contribution made by Marx to the development of socialism was and remains absolutely unique. But Marx was much more than a philosopher. His influence in moving people all over the world to social action ranks him with the founders of the world's greatest faiths. And, like the founders of other faiths, what Marx and others inspired has given millions of people hope, as well as the courage to face persecution and imprisonment.

Since 1917, when the Bolsheviks came to power in the Soviet Union, we have had a great deal of experience of national power structures created in the name of Marxism, and of the achievements and failures of those systems. Some of the sternest critics of Soviet society also based themselves upon Marx, including Leon Trotsky, Mao Tse-tung, Tito and a range of libertarian Marxist dissidents in Eastern Europe and Eurocommunists in the West.

This lecture is concerned with only two aspects of Marxism. *First,* the challenge which Marxism presents to liberal capitalist societies which have achieved a form of political democracy based upon universal adult suffrage; and *second,* the challenge to those societies, which have based themselves on Marxism by the demands for political democracy.

It is, I believe, through a study of this mutual challenge that we can get to the heart of many of the problems now confronting the communist and the non-communist countries, and illuminate the conflicts within and between different economic systems and between the developed and the developing world.

Before I begin, let me make my own convictions clear.

1. I believe that no mature tradition of political democracy today can survive if it does not open itself to the influence of Marx and Marxism.

2. I believe that communist societies cannot survive if they do not accept the demands of the people for democratic rights upon which a secure foundation of consent for socialism must ultimately rest.

3. I believe that world peace can be maintained only if the peoples of the world are discouraged from holding to the false notion that a holy war is necessary between Marxists and non-Marxists.

4. I believe that the moral values upon which social justice must rest require us to accept that Marxism is now a world faith and must be allowed to enter into a continuing dialogue with other world faiths, including religious faiths.

5. I believe that socialism can only prosper if socialists can develop a framework for discussing the full richness of their own traditions and be ready to study the now-considerable history of their own successes and failures.

The evolution of British democracy

If an understanding of socialism begins – as it must – with a scientific study of our own experience, each country can best begin by examining its own history and the struggles of its people for social, economic and political progress.

British socialists can identify many sources from which our ideas have been drawn. The teachings of Jesus, calling upon us to 'Love our neighbour as ourselves' acquired a revolutionary character when preached as a guide to social action. For example, when, in the Peasants' Revolt of 1381, the Reverend John Ball, with his liberation theology, allied himself to a popular uprising, both he, the preacher, and Wat Tyler, the peasant leader, were killed and their followers scattered and crushed by the King.

The message of social justice, equality and democracy is a very old one, and has been carried like a torch from generation to generation by a succession of popular and religious movements, by writers, philosophers, preachers and poets, and has remained a focus of hope, that an alternative society could be constructed. The national political influences of these ideas was seen in the seventeenth, eighteenth, nineteenth and twentieth centuries, and in the revolutions in England, America, France and Russia, each of which provided an important impetus to these hopes. But it was the Industrial Revolution, and the emergence of modern trade unionism in the nineteenth century, which provided a solid foundation of common interest upon which these Utopian dreams could be based, that gave the campaigns for political democracy and social advance their first real chance of success.

If British experience is unique – as it is – in the history of the working-class movement, it lies in the fact that the Industrial Revolution began here, and gave birth to the three main economic philosophies which now dominate the thinking of the world.

The first was capitalism. Adam Smith, in his *Wealth of Nations*, developed the concept of modern capitalism as the best way to release the forces of technology from the dead hand of a declining and corrupted feudalism, substituting the invisible hand of the market and paving the way for industrial expansion and, later, imperialism. The Manchester School of liberal economists and the liberal view of an extended franchise combined to create a power structure which still commands wide support among the Establishment today.

The second was socialism. Robert Owen, the first man specifically identified as a socialist, also developed his ideas of socialism, cooperation and industrial trade unionism out of his experience of the workings of British capitalism.

And the third was Marxism. Marx and Engels also evolved many of their views of scientific socialism from a detailed examination of the nature of British capitalism and the conditions of the working-class movement within it.

Yet, despite the fact that capitalism, socialism and Marxism all first developed in this country, only one of these schools of thought is now accepted by the Establishment as being legitimate. Capitalism, its mechanisms, values and institutions are now being preached with renewed vigour by the British Establishment under the influence of

Milton Friedman. Socialism is attacked as being, at best, romantic or, at worst, destructive. And Marxism is identified as the Antichrist, against which the full weight of official opinion is continually pitted in the propaganda war of ideas.

The distortion of Marxism

The term Marxist is used by the Establishment to prevent it being understood. Even serious writers and broadcasters in the British media use the word 'Marxist' as if it were synonymous with terrorism, violence, espionage, thought control, Russian imperialism and every act of bureaucracy attributable to the state machine in any country, including Britain, which has adopted even the mildest left-of-centre political or social reforms. The effect of this is to isolate Britain from having an understanding of, or a real influence in, the rest of the world, where Marxism is seriously discussed and not drowned by propaganda, as it is in our so-called free press. This ideological insularity harms us all.

This continuing barrage of abuse is maintained at such a high level of intensity that it has obliterated – as is intended – any serious public debate in the mainstream media on what Marxism is about. This negative propaganda is comparable to the treatment accorded to Christianity in non-Christian societies. Any sustained challenge to the existing order that cannot be answered on its merits is dismissed as coming from a Marxist, communist, Trotskyite or extremist. All those suspected of Marxist views run the risk of being listed in police files, having their phones tapped and their career prospects stunted by blacklisting, just as those who advocate liberal ideas will be harassed in the USSR. Those who openly declare their adherence to Marxism are pilloried as self-confessed Marxists, as if they had pleaded guilty to a serious crime and were held in custody awaiting trial.

Even the Labour Party, in which Marxist ideas have had a minority influence, is now described as a Marxist party, as if such a statement of itself put the party beyond the pale of civilised conduct, its arguments required no further answer and its policies are entitled to no proper presentation to the public on the media. One aspect of this propaganda assault which merits notice is that it is mainly waged by those who have never studied Marx, and do not understand what he was saying, or why, yet still regard themselves as highly educated because they have passed all the stages necessary to acquire a university degree. For virtually the whole British Establishment has been, at least until recently, educated without any real knowledge of Marxism, and is determined to see that these ideas do not reach the public. This constitutes a major weakness for the British people as a whole.

Six reasons why Marxism is feared

Why then is Marxism so widely abused? In seeking the answer to that question we shall find the nature of the Marxist challenge in the capitalist democracies. The danger of Marxism is seen by the Establishment to lie in the following characteristics.

First, Marxism is feared because it contains an analysis of an inherent, ineradicable conflict between capital and labour – the theory of the class struggle. Until this theory was first propounded the idea of social class was widely understood and openly discussed by the upper and middle classes, as in England until Victorian times and later.

But when Marx launched the idea of working-class solidarity, as a key to the mobilisation of the forces of social change and the inevitability of victory that that would secure, the term 'class' was conveniently dropped in favour of the idea of national unity, around which there existed a supposed common interest in economic and social advance within our system of society, whether that common interest is real or not. Anyone today who speaks of class in the context of politics runs the risk of excommunication and outlawry. In short, they themselves become casualties in the class war which those who have fired on them claim does not exist.

Second, Marxism is feared because Marx's analysis of capitalism led him to a study of the role of state power as offering a supportive structure of administration, justice and law enforcement, which, far from being objective and impartial in its dealings with the people, was, he argued, in fact an expression of the interests of the established order and the means by which it sustains itself. One recent example of this was Lord Denning's 1980 Dimbleby Lecture. It unintentionally confirmed that interpretation in respect of the judiciary, and is interesting mainly because few twentieth-century judges have been foolish enough to let that cat out of the bag, where it has been quietly hiding for so many years.

Third, Marxism is feared because it provides the trade-union and Labour movement with an analysis of society that inevitably arouses political consciousness, taking it beyond wage militancy within capitalism. The impotence of much American trade unionism and the weakness of past non-political trade unionism in Britain have borne witness to the strength of the argument for a Labour movement with a conscious political perspective that campaigns for the reshaping of society, and does not just compete with its own people for a larger part of a fixed share of money allocated as wages by those who own capital, and who continue to decide what that share will be.

Fourth, Marxism is feared because it is international in outlook, appeals widely to working people everywhere, and contains within its internationalism a potential that is strong enough to defeat imperialism, neo-colonialism and multinational business and finance, which have always organised internationally. But international capital has fended off the power of international labour by resorting to cynical appeals to nationalism by stirring up suspicion and hatred against outside enemies. This fear of Marxism has been intensified since 1917 by the claim that all international Marxism stems from the Kremlin, whose interests all Marxists are alleged to serve slavishly, thus making them, according to capitalist Establishment propaganda, the witting or unwitting agents of the national interest of the USSR.

Fifth, Marxism is feared because it is seen as a threat to the older organised religions, as expressed through their hierarchies and temporal power structures, and their close alliance with other manifestations of state and economic power. The political establishments of the West, which for centuries have openly worshipped money and profit and ignored the fundamental teachings of Jesus, do, in fact, sense in Marxism a moral challenge to their shallow and corrupted values and it makes them very uncomfortable. Ritualised and mystical religious teachings, which offer advice to the rich to be good and the poor to be patient, each seeking personal salvation in this world and eternal life in the next, are also liable to be unsuccessful in the face of such a strong moral challenge as socialism makes.

There have, over the centuries, always been some Christians who, remembering the teachings of Jesus, have espoused these ideas, and today there are many radical Christians who have joined hands with working people in their struggles. The liberation theology of Latin America proves this, and thus deepens the anxieties of Church and State in the West.

Sixth, Marxism is feared in Britain precisely because it *is* believed by many in the Establishment to be capable of winning consent for radical change through its influence in the trade-union movement, and then in the election of socialist candidates through the ballot box. It is indeed therefore because the Establishment believes in the real possibility of an advance of Marxist ideas by fully democratic means that they have had to devote so much time and effort to the misrepresentation of Marxism as a philosophy of violence and destruction, to scare people away from listening to what Marxists have to say.

These six fears, which are both expressed and fanned by those who defend a particular social order, actually pinpoint the wide appeal of Marxism, its durability and its strength more accurately than many advocates of Marxism may appreciate.

Marxism and the Labour Party

The *Communist Manifesto*, and many other works of Marxist philosophy, have always profoundly influenced the British Labour movement and the British Labour Party, and have strengthened our understanding and enriched our thinking.

It would be as unthinkable to try to construct the Labour Party without Marx as it would be to establish university faculties of astronomy, anthropology or psychology without permitting the study of Copernicus, Darwin or Freud, and still expect such faculties to be taken seriously.

There is also a practical reason for emphasising this point now. The attacks upon the so-called hard left of the Labour Party by its opponents in the Conservative, Liberal and Social Democratic Parties and by the Establishment, are not motivated by fear of the influence of Marxists alone. These attacks are really directed at all socialists and derive from the knowledge that democratic socialism in all its aspects does reflect the true interest of a majority of people in this country, and that what democratic socialists are saying is getting through to more and more people, despite the round-the-clock efforts of the media to fill the newspapers and the airwaves with a cacophony of distortion.

If the Labour Party could be bullied or persuaded to denounce its Marxists, the media – having tasted blood – would demand next that it expelled all its socialists and reunited the remaining Labour Party with the SDP to form a harmless alternative to the Conservatives, which could then be allowed to take office now and again when the Conservatives fell out of favour with the public. Thus British capitalism, it is argued, would be made safe for ever, and socialism would be squeezed off the national agenda. But if such a strategy were to succeed – which it will not – it would in fact profoundly endanger British society. For it would open up the danger of a swing to the far right, as we have seen in Europe over the last fifty years.

Weaknesses of the Marxist position

But having said all that about the importance of the Marxist critique, let me turn to the Marxist remedies for the ills that Marx so accurately diagnosed. There are many schools of thought within the Marxist tradition, and it would be as foolish to lump them all together as to bundle every Christian denomination into one and then seek to generalise about the faith. Nevertheless, there are certain aspects of the central Marxist analysis which it is necessary to subject to special scrutiny if the relationship between Marxism and democracy is to be explored.

I have listed some of these aspects because of their relevance to this lecture, and which explain in part why I would not think it correct to call myself a Marxist.

Marx seemed to identify *all* social and personal morality as being a product of economic forces, thus denying to that morality any objective existence over and above the inter-relationship of social and economic forces at that moment in history. I cannot accept that analysis.

Of course the laws, customs, administration, armed forces and received wisdom in any society will tend to reflect the interests and values of the dominant class, and if class relationships change by technology, evolution or revolution, this will be reflected in a change of the social and cultural superstructure. But to go beyond that and deny the *inherent* rights of men and women to live, to think, to act, to argue or to obey or resist in pursuit of some inner call of conscience – as pacifists do – or to codify their relationships with each other in terms of moral responsibility, seems to me to be throwing away the child of moral teaching with the dirty bath-water of feudalism, capitalism or clericalism.

In saying this, I am consciously seeking to re-establish the relevance and legitimacy of the moral teachings of Jesus, whilst accepting that many manifestations of episcopal authority and ritualistic escapism have blanked out that essential message of human brotherhood and sisterhood. I say this for many reasons.

First, because without some concept of inherent human rights and moral values and obligations, derived by custom and practice out of the accumulated experience of our societies, I cannot see any valid reason why socialism should have any moral force behind it, or how socialism can relate directly to the human condition outside economic relationships; for example, as between women and men, black and white, or in the relationships within the home and in personal life.

Second, because I regard the moral pressures released by radical Christian teaching, and its humanistic offshoots, as having played a major role in developing the ideas of solidarity, democracy, equality and peace which have contributed to the development of socialist motivation.

Third, because without the acceptance of a strong moral code, the ends always can be argued to justify the means, and this lies at the root of some of the oppression which has been practised in actually existing socialist societies.

Fourth, because the teachings of Marx, like the teachings of Jesus, can also become obscured, lost and even reversed by civil-power systems established in states that proclaim themselves to be Marxist, just as many Christian kings and governors destroyed, by their actions, the faith they asserted they were sworn to defend. And if Jesus is to be acquitted of any responsibility for the tortures and murders conducted by the Inquisition, so must Marx be exonerated from any charges arising from the imprisonment and executions that occurred in Stalin's Russia.

Fifth, because without a real moral impulse and a warm human compassion, I cannot find any valid reason why Marx himself should have devoted so much of his time to works of scholarship and endless political activities, all of which were designed to achieve better conditions for his fellow creatures. That, no doubt, is why Marx is sometimes regarded as the last of the Old Testament prophets.

If I am asked where these moral imperatives come from, if not from the interaction of economic forces, my answer would be that they spring from the wells of human genius interacting upon our experience of life, which were also the sources of inspiration for Marx in his work.

It is very important for many reasons that religion and politics should not be separated into watertight compartments, forever at war with each other. For centuries the central social arguments and battles which we now see as political or economic were conducted under the heading of religion. Many of the most important popular struggles were conceived by those who participated in them as being waged in pursuit of religious convictions. Similarly, some of the most oppressive political establishments exercised their power in the name of God.

Unless we are prepared to translate the religious vocabulary which served as a vehicle for political ideas for so many centuries into a modern vocabulary that recognises the validity of a scientific analysis both of nature, society and its economic interests, we shall cut ourselves off from all those centuries of human struggle and experience and deny ourselves the richness of our own inheritance.

Marx and Marxist historians have, of course, consciously reinterpreted ancient history in the light of their own analysis, but no real dictionary can be restricted to a one-way translation based upon hindsight. We need a two-way translation to enable us to understand and utilise, if we wish to do so, the wisdom of earlier years to criticise contemporary society. It is in this context that I find some other aspects of Marxism unsatisfactory.

Marx made much of the difference between scientific socialism and Utopian socialism, which he believed suffered from its failure to root itself in a vigorous study of the economic and political relationships between the social classes. The painstaking scholarship which he and Engels brought to bear upon capitalism has left us with a formidable set of analytical tools, without which socialists today would have a much poorer theoretical understanding of the tasks which they are undertaking.

But having recognised that priceless analytic legacy that we owe to Marx, in one sense Marx himself was a Utopian, in that he appeared to believe that when capitalism had been replaced by socialism, and socialism by communism, a classless society, liberated by the final withering away of the State, would establish some sort of heaven on earth. Human experience does not, unfortunately, give us many grounds for sharing that optimism. For humanity cannot organise itself without some power structure of the State, and Marx seems to have underestimated the importance of Lord Acton's warning that power 'tends to corrupt', mistakenly believing this danger would disappear under communism.

Morality, accountability and the British Labour movement

It is here that both the moral argument referred to above, and the issue of democratic accountability, which have both played so large a part in the pre-Marxist and non-Marxist traditions of the British Labour movement, can be seen to have such relevance.

For allowing for the weaknesses of Labourism, economism and the anti-theoretical pragmatism which have characterised the British working-class movement at its worst, two of the beliefs to which our movement has clung most doggedly were the idea that some actions were 'right' and others were 'wrong'; and the obstinate determination to force those exercising political or economic power over us to accept the ultimate discipline of accountability, up to now seen mainly through the regular use of the ballot box, through which all adults would have their say in a universal suffrage to elect or dismiss governments.

The British working-class movement has over the years clung passionately to these twin ideas of morality and accountability in politics and they constitute the backbone of our faith. Some Marxists might argue that these objectives are too limited, are not specifically socialist and constitute little more than a cover for collaborationist strategies which underpin bourgeois capitalist liberal democracy, complete with its soothing religious tranquillisers. I readily admit that a humanitarian morality and accountability are not enough, in themselves, to establish socialism, but they are essential if socialism is to be established, and if socialism is to be worth having at all. A socialist economic transformation may be achieved by force, but if so, it then cannot be sustained by agreement, and socialism may degenerate into the imposition of a regime administered by those whose attempts to maintain it can actually undermine it rather than develop it.

The issue of parliamentary democracy

How then, on this analysis, should we approach the arguments between the Marxist and some non-Marxist socialists, which have in the past centred around their different assessment of the importance that should be attached to the role of parliamentary democracy?

Before we can do that we have to examine, in some detail, what is meant by the phrase parliamentary democracy, for it lends itself to many definitions. Seen from the viewpoint of the Establishment, Britain has enjoyed parliamentary government since 1295. All that has happened in the intervening period is that the Queen-in-Parliament has agreed to exercise the Crown's powers constitutionally.

This means accepting legislation passed 'by and with the advice and consent of the Lords Spiritual and Temporal in Parliament assembled', and accepting that an elected majority in the House of Commons is entitled to expect that its leader will be asked to form an administration by the Crown; and that that administration will be composed of Her Majesty's ministers, who in their capacity as Crown advisers will be free to use the Royal prerogatives to administer and control the civil and military services of the Crown.

These democratic advances are circumscribed in four significant respects.

First, in practice by the actual problems confronting an elected Labour government in establishing democratic control over the highly secretive self-directing and hierarchical executive of state power.

Second, by the constitutional power of the Crown to dismiss a government and dissolve a parliament at any time.

Third, by the fact that a government so dismissed, and a parliament so dissolved, lose all legal rights over the state machine and all legislative powers.

Fourth, by the subordination of all United Kingdom legislation, even when it has received the royal assent, to the superior authority of Common Market law or court judgements, which take precedence, under the European Communities Act, over domestic legislation, where the two conflict. It is worth noting that British accession to the EEC involved, in this sense, a major diminution of the powers of the Crown, in that royal assent to legislation rendered invalid by the EEC is itself invalid.

Set out baldly like that, it can be seen that in a formal sense Britain is far less democratic in its form of government than those countries whose peoples may elect a president, both Houses of their legislature and have entrenched their rights in written constitutional safeguards. Why then does the British Labour movement appear to be so satisfied with our democratic institutions?

In one sense, of course, it is not. The abolition of the House of Lords and the abrogation of British accession to the Treaty of Rome are amongst the items likely to feature high on the agenda for the next Labour manifesto.

The Labour Party just assumes that the Crown will always act with scrupulous care within the constitutional conventions that govern the use of the prerogative, and for that reason have never put this issue on its political agenda. Beyond that, Labour believes that the reality of power precludes the possibility that our democratic rights might be overturned by an abnormal use of those formal powers which still reside in the non-elected elements of our constitution.

In sharp contrast to the Establishment view, Labour's broad interpretation of the parliamentary democracy we have secured is that, by a succession of extra-parliamentary struggles over the centuries, the Crown was made accountable to Parliament, the Lords were made subordinate to the Commons, and the Commons were, through regular election, subordinated to the will of the electorate, made up first of men and later of women too, who have won (in fact, if not yet in constitutional theory) the sovereign rights which belong to the people – which is what democracy is all about.

It is manifestly true that such an achievement, formidable as it is, falls short of a constitutional entrenchment of the sovereignty of the people, and that it secures no more than the right to dismiss governments and MPs and substitute new MPs and new governments. It certainly does not offer, of itself, any control over the extra-parliamentary centres of financial or economic power, which remain whichever government has been elected, or even guarantee ministerial or parliamentary power over the apparatus of the State. To that extent, democracy in Britain is still partial and political, but not economic or social.

But if, as I believe, the real strength of parliamentary democracy lies in the fact that the power to remove governments without violent revolution is now vested in the people, that is a very significant gain, which should not be dismissed as being of little account, a fraud to be exposed, bypassed and replaced.

One of the reasons why the British Labour Party and the British people are so suspicious of certain supposedly revolutionary schools of Marxist thought is that they believe that insufficient attention is paid by them to the importance of our democratic institutions, thus defined; and fear that if they were to be dismantled, we should lose what we struggled so hard and so long to achieve. We would then be set back, perhaps with no gains to show for it. Parliamentary democracy is an evolving system, not yet fully developed, which enjoys wide support for what it has achieved so far.

The myth of revolutionary activity in Britain

Given the fact that all our rights in Parliament have been won by struggle, I must add that I have not observed any serious revolutionary movements pledged to destroy Parliament anywhere across the whole spectrum of socialist parties of the left in Britain today.

Those who call themselves revolutionary socialists and denounce the rest of us as nothing more than left-talking reformists are not, in my judgement, real revolutionaries at all. They are nothing more than left-talking revolutionists who, while pointing to the deficiencies in our parliamentary democracy, offer themselves as candidates for Parliament, and none of them are planning an armed revolution or a general strike to secure power by a *coup d'état*. If such people do exist, I have not met them, heard of them, or become aware of any influence they have in any known political party or grouping of the left.

Nor, for that matter, is there much hard evidence to suggest that there would be wide public support for a counter-revolution to topple an elected Labour Government by force, on the Chilean model.

I appreciate that in playing down some of the most cherished fears of both ultra-left and ultra-right I am laying myself open to a charge of naïvety, and depriving the mass media of one of their favourite and most spine-chilling horror myths, which they use to undermine public support for socialism.

If there ever were to be a right-wing coup in Britain, it would not be carried out by paratroopers landing in central London – as it once seemed they would land in Paris just before de Gaulle came to power – but by an attempt to repeat what happened to Gough Whitlam when the Governor General dismissed him as Prime Minister.

And if the Labour movement and the left were ever to resort to force in Britain, it would not be to overthrow an elected government, but to prevent the overthrow of an elected government – i.e. in defence of, and not in defiance of, parliamentary democracy. It is, in this sense, and only in this sense, that the use of popular force would ever be contemplated by the Labour and socialist movements.

The role of extra-parliamentary activity

Though these may seem to be highly theoretical matters, it is necessary, to complete the analysis, to refer briefly to the varying circumstances in which popular action is legitimate.

There is clearly an inherent right to take up arms against tyranny or dictatorship, to establish or uphold democracy, on exactly the same basis, and for the same reasons, that the nation will respond to a call to arms to defeat a foreign invasion, or repel those who have successfully occupied a part of our territory.

In a different context, we accept certain more limited rights to defy the law on grounds of conscience, or to resist laws that threaten basic and long-established liberties, as for example if Parliament were to prolong its life and remove the electoral rights of its citizens. The defence of ancient and inherent rights, as for example the rights of women, or of trade unionists, or of minority communities, could legitimately lead to some limited civil disobedience, accompanied by an assertion that the responsibility for it rested upon those who had removed these rights in the first place. And, at the very opposite end of this scale of legitimate opposition, lies the undoubted right to act directly to bring public pressure, from outside Parliament, to bear upon Parliament to secure a redress of legitimate grievances. Such extra-parliamentary activity has played a long and honourable part in the endless struggle to win basic rights.

To assert that extra-parliamentary activity is synonymous with anti-parliamentary conspiracies is to blur a distinction that it is essential to draw with scientific precision, if we are to understand what is happening and not mistake a democratic demonstration for an undemocratic riot; a democratic protest for an undemocratic uprising; or a democratic reformer for an undemocratic revolutionary.

The Labour movement in Britain, egged on by a hostile media, is now engaged in a microscopic examination of its own attitude to the role of extra-parliamentary activity. Such an examination can only help to advance socialism. Perhaps the simplest way to understand these issues is to examine the attitude of the Conservative Party to the same issues. The Tory Party and its historical predecessors have never wasted a moment's valuable time upon such constitutional niceties. Throughout our whole history, the owners of land, the banks and our industries, have been well aware that their power lay almost entirely outside Parliament, and their interest in Parliament was confined to a determination to maintain a majority there, to safeguard their interests by legislating to protect them. Extra-parliamentary activity has been a way of life for the ruling classes, from the Restoration, through to the overthrow of the 1931 Labour Government and the election in 1979 of Mrs Thatcher.

In power they use Parliament to protect their class interests and reward their friends. In opposition they use the Lords, where they always have a majority, to frustrate the Labour majority in the Commons, and supplement this with a sustained campaign of extra-parliamentary activity to undermine the power of Labour governments by investment strikes, attacks upon the pound sterling, granting or withholding business confidence – all using, when necessary, the power of the IMF, the multinationals and the media.

Labour has real power outside Parliament, and the people we represent can only look to an advance of their interests and of the prospects of socialism if Labour MPs harness themselves to the movement outside and develop a strong partnership, which alone can infuse fresh life into Parliament as an agent of democratic change.

These matters and the associated issues of party democracy have received a great deal of attention within the Labour movement over the last few years and it is not hard to see why. We want the Labour

Party to practise the accountability it preaches. Seen in that light, the adherence of the labour movement to parliamentary democracy, and our determination to expand it, becomes a great deal more than a romantic attachment to liberal capitalist bourgeois institutions. By contrast, it can be seen to have a crucial role to play in achieving greater equality and economic democracy.

————————◄○►————————

Friday 30 July 1982

I feel somehow that we are at a real turning point in politics. I can't quite describe it. The military victory in the Falklands War, Thatcher's strength, the counter-attack of the right of the Labour Party on the left, the fact that unemployment has weakened the unions, and so on, make me feel more than ever before that I need to pause and think and work out a new strategy. Caroline has persuaded me that the press assassination of me was successful and that I've lived in a dream world believing it wasn't really happening. The NEC is in a bitter state, set on expulsions, ASLEF was sold down the river by the TUC, and even if they hadn't been I'm not sure how long they could have survived the Chairman of BR, Sir Peter Parker. The media are now in an absolutely hysterical state. I feel we have just come to the end of an era.

Saturday 25 September 1982
Labour Party Conference, Blackpool

Compared to last year, when the left was riding high with success everywhere, this year the left is very much tail-between-legs. We did unleash a violent backlash from the right supported by the media and the general secretaries, and although the Party is pretty solid on policy it doesn't want divisions, so we are caught by the constraint of unity – whereas they, being on the warpath, are not, and are demanding the expulsion of the left. It's very unpleasant but I shall just let it ride over me; at this stage we have to accept that the right have won and there isn't much we can do about it.

--------◄○►--------

Despite the military victory of the British in the Falklands War of 1982, Tony Benn and Tam Dalyell and a small group of MPs, though much vilified, continued their opposition to the prosecution of the war and tried to expose its aftermath. In December 1982, in the Chamber of the House of Commons, Tony reiterated his opposition to the expedition.

Millions of people in Britain of many political allegiances, and of none, opposed the task force and the government's handling of the situation in the Falklands from the beginning. It is right that our voice should be heard in this debate.

The real lessons of this tragic and unnecessary war are not dealt with in the White Paper, which is little more than part of the campaign for a bigger defence budget. The Secretary of State spoke of world affairs as if they could be thought of, primarily, in military terms. In some cases, he spoke as if war has already broken out.

The real lessons of the Falklands are political, not military. The first lesson is that the future of the Falklands should have been settled years ago by negotiations under the auspices of the United Nations, as the United Nations decided it should be on 16 December 1965. All governments – two Conservative and two Labour – since 1965 can be criticised for not taking those negotiations seriously. For example, the Argentine claim and its historical basis have never been presented to Parliament or to the British people as having any serious basis. That is not the view of the majority of the United Nations.

Secondly, Parliament and the public were never told of the islands' dependence for their life support upon Argentina in respect of trade, transport, education and health. The true cost of replacing that support is only now becoming apparent. Successive governments have failed to think through the future of those outposts of Empire such as the Falklands, Hong Kong and Gibraltar, which have been left as anachronisms in our post-imperial circumstances.

The real responsibility of the House should be limited to the protection of the people who live there, and not based on the protection of the territories themselves.

The armed invasion by Argentina, which was a clear breach of international law and which the United Nations recognised as such, drew from the government the first serious British peace proposals. These were published on 20 May and withdrawn on the same day. I have alluded to those proposals before. I shall refer to them again briefly.

The government, the Cabinet and the Prime Minister published those proposals for a mutual military withdrawal, or a United Nations administration with British and Argentine participation, and for real negotiations under the United Nations about the sovereignty and administration of the islands. If those proposals had been offered at any time since 1965, they would have settled the issue without bloodshed. They would have carried the full support of the United Nations, and still would. The House should not forget that they will have to form the basis for any permanent settlement.

Instead of following that course, the government deliberately chose a military solution. To justify the war, they adopted a policy that has brought discredit on the government and on Britain.

[SIR JOHN BIGGS-DAVISON: 'It was General Galtieri who chose a military solution.']

I am sorry, but the hon. Gentleman has not been listening to what I have said. I was saying that if the government's peace proposals of 20 May had been advanced at any time in the past seventeen years, the matter could have been settled without bloodshed.

The proposals that the government issued on 20 May deliberately left the issue of sovereignty open. My right hon. Friend the Member for Cardiff South-East, who was once Foreign Secretary, will know – as will every other Foreign Secretary since 1965 – that they would very much have liked an agreement with Argentina, but that one of the factors involved was fear of public criticism if they were to come out openly with the plans that were known to be in discussion in the Foreign Office.

I should like to deal with the way in which the government justified the military action that they took. The first argument was that it was a war against Fascism, but they armed the junta right up to the last moment. They supported a fascist junta in Chile, just as they supported fascist governments all over the world.

Even now, the government appear to be assenting to a big bank loan to the Argentine Government.

The government pretended that the task force was sent to strengthen our hand in negotiations, but from the start it was intended to reoccupy the islands by force.

The third lesson is that the government have isolated Britain in the world by their actions. There was full United Nations support for Britain on 3 April, but after the 4 November debate in the United Nations, even the United States was on the other side. The Hispanic world has remained united against us, France and Germany – our major partners in the EC – have renewed arms supplies to Argentina, and British communities all over Latin America have been in danger.

The fourth lesson is that, in the process, the government have undermined the role of the United Nations as a peace-maker, when our only real hope of avoiding a nuclear war is by international action under the United Nations.

The fifth lesson is that the government committed hundreds of millions of pounds – probably billions of pounds – to an enterprise that is doomed to fail, in that Argentina will, in the end, acquire a leading position in the control of the Falklands. The figure now quoted – we have only been allowed the information in dribs and drabs – is £2 billion to £3 billion. Each year, £400 million – more than £1 million a day – is to be spent on the garrison. A further £30 million to £35 million has been allocated for development. Between £1 million and £2 million per Falkland islander has been spent on this enterprise, the lessons of which the retiring Secretary of State says are only military. The government caused untold human suffering for those courageous men who died, and for the families whose sons were killed or maimed in an enterprise that cannot achieve its prime purpose.

I shall go further and say what I know will not be popular among Conservative Members. I deeply feel, as do others, that the government used the sacrifices of the dead and wounded to boost the political standing of the Conservative Party in general, and of the Prime Minister in particular. [HON. MEMBERS: 'Disgraceful.'] They invented and exploited the 'Falklands factor', and it has been paid for in blood and bereavement. That view is widely shared throughout the country.

The next charge that I level against the Cabinet is that it deliberately released the poison of militarism into our society. They praised war and killing, and suggested that that dangerous virus was the best remedy for our national ills and that it would in some way restore our pride and self-confidence. In that campaign to reawaken militarism in Britain, Fleet Street, the BBC and the ITN played a considerable part in spreading the poison.

I have made grave charges against the government, but more and more people in Britain know that those charges are true, and the verdict of history will confirm them. After all that has happened, the government have failed because everyone in the world knows that in the end the Falkland Islands will go to Argentina, just as China will recover Hong Kong and Spain will recover Gibraltar, however many warships and aircraft we build.

There are, however, two more hopeful lessons to be learned for the future. First, nuclear weapons were unusable in this case, and will be in any modern war, because no country dares to use them. There is no doubt that there were nuclear weapons on board the ships, despite the government's denials, but even if the Argentine army had secured a military success, those weapons could not have been used.

The second point has a broader political bearing. If all the money, the human effort and the planning by governments that now go into war were devoted to fighting poverty, disease, ignorance and injustice, those scourges could be ended once and for all in Britain and throughout the world. That argument is well understood by many people who do not follow detailed defence debates. If the QE2 can be requisitioned to take troops to the South Atlantic, it can be used to take food to the starving peoples of Asia. The methods of war can be used to meet the underlying problems of people in this country and throughout the world.

Let anyone who doubts that recall that in 1945, after the horrors of the Second World War, the British people chose peace, reconstruction and social justice and rejected Mr Churchill, who was arguably the greatest war leader in our history. I believe that the British people will act in the same way when the real lessons of the Falklands tragedy sink in, and in so doing they will reject the leadership of the present Prime Minister, who has inflicted so much suffering on our people and so gravely damaged our national interest.

◀◇▶

Labour Party Conference, 1982

… Somehow we have to find ways of making the wide diversity of views within the Party into a source of strength, and allow us in that way to stretch out and build a broad alliance of support for victory.

Now I want to tell this Conference plainly, and with no doubt about it, that I pledge myself wholeheartedly and without any reservation whatever to work for the election of a Labour Government under the leadership of Michael Foot; to implement these policies which we have agreed.

And I believe that the whole party and all those who look to us want to know that that is so. Now we must campaign to take this message out to the British people with passion and commitment, to keep it plain and simple; maybe the details of how we do it and the committees and the structures have to be there, so we know how we're going to do it. But we are there to represent people with needs that are not met.

And I believe we shall best win this battle, which is a historic battle for the future of our country, if we arm ourselves with a weapon we have allowed to go rusty in the scabbard. Which is the moral appeal, to a nation; to point out that it is wrong to starve the Health Service to build the Trident; that it is wrong to let old people die of hypothermia, having closed the pits that could give them energy to keep them warm in the winter; that it is wrong to condemn young people to the scrapheap, when we live in a country with so much to do.

Comrades, we are a moral crusade. What we are fighting are not individuals, not even the structures of a system that has failed – we are fighting rotten, decaying values, with better values, of decency, justice and hope, and with those we shall win next time!

—◄◦►—

Monday 13 June 1983

I ordered some stationery because I have been using House of Commons letter-heading for thirty-three years and I haven't even got any with my name and address. The cost of stamps is astronomical; at this present rate, assuming I get 1,000 letters a week, it would cost £120 on stamps alone. I did enquire about my redundancy pay, and I think I get £14,000 tax-free, and a couple of months' winding-up allowance. I'm keeping Julie on. I had a letter from Richard Gott of the *Guardian* inviting me to write a column every week, which will mean £175 a week coming in.

Wednesday 4 January 1984

Arkady Maslennikov, the London correspondent of *Pravda*, came to interview me. He had said he would very much like to see how my computer worked, so, before he arrived, I prepared 'a message from the Central Committee of the CP in Moscow to the London *Pravda* correspondent'. The message stated that it was amazing that he was still using a typewriter, which was a tsarist invention, that he might even be using a medieval instrument known as a pen, that all correspondents had to equip themselves with computers in order to demonstrate the Soviet lead in technology, and 'would he please confirm the receipt of this message by sending a carrier pigeon at once to Moscow'. Maslennikov laughed heartily when I called up the message on the screen. Then I showed him how it could be printed in various typefaces, and he took four copies away with him.

◄○►

A week after Tony Benn was elected MP for Chesterfield, in a by-election on 1 March 1984, the miners' strike, which was to last for a year, began, and he spent much of that year in Derbyshire and Yorkshire and at other coal pits, actively supporting the local miners' unions and the NUM – on soup runs, on marches, visiting jailed miners and appearing on radio and television to combat the predominantly hostile coverage of the strike. Here, in Parliament, he assesses the Conservative plans for the coal industry and the miners' unions.

My first task is to congratulate my hon. Friend the Member for Cynon Valley [Mrs Clwyd] on a most remarkable maiden speech. She spoke with great knowledge, passion and feeling, and represents an area where support for the miners is far greater than Conservative Members begin to understand. They will win the vote in the Division Lobbies tonight, but I venture to tell Conservative Members that they will be defeated by the National Union of Mineworkers and by the people who support it, for reasons that I shall give as briefly as I can.

The hon. Member for Rochford [Dr Clark] referred to the police. What the hon. Gentleman said encourages me to read a letter that I have received from someone who was present at the Mansfield rally a few weeks ago. The writer says: 'I saw two men bedecked in NUM stickers actually pick up a stone each and throw them at the police lines, inciting other miners to do the same and, as in all large rallies there is a hooligan element, some followed suit; as they did so, the first two turned round and announced that they were plain-clothed police officers and tried to arrest one of the miners, but he escaped after intervention by other miners, and the officers were assaulted. Not only did they deserve it, but it is they who should be charged with inciting a riot, not the miners.'

Conservative Members may not have seen what has really been happening. The press reports of what has been happening on the picket lines have completely left out of account the deliberate police provocation of miners. The coverage has been such that people have not realised what has been happening.

I am sorry that the Secretary of State has gone. One had to listen to his speech very carefully to understand that he has made three major changes from the policy of the 'Plan for Coal'. First, the production targets are to be cut from 130 million tonnes next year –rising to 170 million to 200 million tonnes at the end of the century – to less than 100 million tonnes, which is what MacGregor wants. To make a lot of speeches in the House and indulge in point-scoring while failing to tell the House that the government are planning to cut the production of coal in Britain is totally misleading.

The second thing that ministers have not yet been honest enough to admit – we may have to rely on another leak – is that they intend to sell off the profitable pits. That is why they are investing in Selby. They want to pour public money into Selby and some of the Nottinghamshire coalfields so that when they have beaten the NUM – as they think that they will, but they will not – they can sell off the pits into which they have poured public money. [AN HON. MEMBER: 'Rubbish.'] The hon.

Gentleman says, 'Rubbish.' But it is government policy to sell off the oil, BT, the airways, the railways and the pits. If the hon. Gentleman wishes to say, 'Rubbish', let him say it to his own front bench.

The third point which was not made plain in the Secretary of State's speech – and I am not surprised about that – was that the whole objective of the Government is to isolate and defeat the NUM. Everyone knows that throughout the time when Labour was in office there was the closest consultation between the NUM, the NCB and the government. My right hon. Friend the Member for Salford East [Mr Orme], my hon. Friend the Member for Midlothian [Mr Eadie] and I were all involved. The present government have excluded the NUM from any meaningful discussions about the future of the industry.

That is why there was an immediate response at Cortonwood. When the Secretary of State says that there will be no compulsory redundancies, how can anyone believe him? Those who moved to Cortonwood were told that there would be five years' work there. They were then given five weeks' notice of the closure. The miners do not believe a word ministers say, and they are absolutely right.

I turn to the economic argument. We produce the cheapest deep-mined coal in the world. If subsidies in Britain were the same as those in the Common Market, the NCB would make a profit of £2 billion a year. Agriculture is subsidised up to the hilt. Indeed, the dairy farmers – including all the dairy farmers in the House – are up in arms if their subsidy is temporarily and momentarily eroded by a government which has poured money into uneconomic land. Candidly, I am in favour of keeping our land in use for food production, just as I am in favour of keeping our pits in use for future energy for the nation.

People talk about cheaper South African coal. What about the wages of the South African miners? Mr Botha – that friend of Hitler who was invited to Chequers to celebrate, no doubt, the fortieth anniversary of D-Day – represents a coal industry which will not allow unions to exist and pays the miners a pittance. Yet we are told that we must be competitive with that industry.

[MR MARLOW: What about Australian coal?]

When the present Secretary of State, the right hon. Member for Worcester [Mr Walker], was in charge of the industry in 1973, he ordered Australian coal. When we were in power in 1974, the Australian coal arrived. It was so expensive that the Central Electricity Generating Board sold it at a loss to Électricité de France, because it was more expensive than British coal. I remember that very well.

We are told about the necessity to be economic. What about nuclear power? No private financier has ever put a penny into nuclear power. It has been subsidised from the beginning. The reason why a pressurised water reactor is to be built and why the government, in advance of the Layfield inquiry, have authorised the spending of £200 million is that the Americans want the plutonium for their Cruise-missile warheads. It has now been admitted in the newspapers, after reports in Congress, that the American Government cannot persuade their own people to build nuclear-power stations and are therefore relying on British plutonium to maintain their warheads.

Those are the realities of the economics. The costs of the closures are greater than the costs of investment, and the cost of the strike makes economic nonsense of the government's case.

The other argument is that the government's policy is a continuation of Labour policy. Our investment programme under the 'Plan for Coal' was for 170 million to 200 million tonnes by the end of the century. The target is now to be under 100 million tonnes. Every item of policy, including closures, was discussed and agreed by us with the NUM. As Secretary of State for Energy, I offered the NUM executive a veto on all closures, in order to be sure that the NUM, the NCB and the government would be able to agree to produce the coal.

There has been a great deal of hypocrisy about the government not intervening. They are deeply involved. The police are preventing peaceful picketing. They have set up road blocks, introduced curfews in the villages and provoked on the picket lines. There have been cavalry charges against unarmed pickets. That is a disgrace to the British police, for which the government are responsible. This afternoon I asked in the House about the use of troops, and the Leader of the House was very evasive. At the beginning of the dispute I asked the Leader of the House whether the armed forces had been alerted, and he gave a categorical assurance that they had not. Now the Prime Minister has written to me. I had asked her whether the troops were involved. She used a very skilful phrase. She said that there has been no authorisation. She did not say that the troops were not being used, and she admitted that the army and the armed forces are supplying facilities and transport as part of a joint police and military operation. Either the Leader of the House or the Prime Minister was misleading the House.

The magistrates have come in and introduced bail conditions that amount to a sentence – a sort of exclusion zone – for those who have been convicted of nothing. Much has been made of the crudity of the way in which the government have turned off every source of funds, including social security, to starve the miners back to work. They have 'deemed' that the miners have been getting strike pay, when in fact they have not. They have cut maternity grants and excluded from strike pay workers who have been only indirectly involved and were never employees of the NCB. One case that came to my attention was of the government stopping a retired miner benefiting from the redundancy payment scheme because, for a short while, he was on the NCB's books before the strike began.

The miners know that the large sums of money that are given to them are not real money. They are a lump-sum payment for future social-security benefits, as they will not get those benefits until the redundancy pay has been spent. Neither the tightening of the screw through the Department of Health and Social Security nor the attempted bribery through redundancy pay will affect the miners.

The most remarkable thing that has occurred in the coalfields is that the miners are fighting the present policy and will go on doing so, and the government can do nothing whatever to stop them. Young miners know full well that if, at twenty-nine or thirty, they take the money that is offered, there will be no work for them, their children or their grandchildren in the areas in which they live. They will not accept it. It is a most vivid example of the non-nuclear defence strategy. When people are fighting for something in which they believe, they will make many more sacrifices than the policemen waving their £600-a-week pay slips at the picket lines to provoke the miners. The women are supporting the miners as has never happened before, and many have been arrested.

I believe that the leadership of Arthur Scargill and the NUM executive has been brilliant throughout the dispute. The Secretary of State has returned. He lost his job as Secretary of State for Trade and Industry by mishandling the miners, and he will lose his job again because he is up against a National Union of Mineworkers that has been warning people for years about what the NCB and the government want. I heard Arthur Scargill at the Durham Miners' Gala three or four years ago describing the hit list of pits. Even Joe Gormley, who is now in another place, denounced what he said, but every word that Arthur Scargill said was true. That is why miners support him. They are also getting enormous support—

[MR MARLOW: Why not have a ballot then?]

Conservative Members destroyed trade unionism at Cheltenham without a ballot and intend to take away votes in metropolitan counties without a vote. They cannot suddenly pretend that they are in favour of a ballot in a national dispute. Eighty-seven per cent of the miners are on strike, and will remain on strike until the dispute ends. The financial and other support, such as food, that is being given to the miners and mining areas is on a scale of which there is no parallel in any industrial dispute in living memory. The money and the food are pouring in.

I have attended ten or twenty meetings on the European elections and every one of them has concerned the miners. No one should think that when 14 June comes it will not be the miners who are in people's minds, when they vote Labour against the government and all that they stand for. I believe that the miners are getting such support because they are fighting for all of us. They are fighting to preserve local government, for public services and for the women at Greenham Common in such a way as to attract the support of the overwhelming majority of the Labour movement.

The government were wrong in 1926. They were wrong again in 1972 and capitulated. They were wrong in 1974 and were defeated. This miners' strike will send the Secretary of State into his final retirement, because they are fighting for the country's future and its energy supplies, which are now threatened once again by the Gulf War and are not to be entrusted to the private oil companies. When the House divides, I do not doubt that it will carry the government's amendment. However, the government will not carry the support of the British people, who are overwhelmingly behind the NUM in its struggle.

Thursday 1 March 1984,
day of the Chesterfield by-election

The *Sun* had an article, 'Benn on the Couch' – a top psychiatrist's view of 'Britain's leading leftie' – in which they said they had fed my personal and political details to a psychiatrist in America who had concluded that I was power-hungry, would do anything to satisfy my hunger, was prone to periods of fantasy, and so on.

There were rowdy scenes when we got onto the platform, all the young people came in chanting, 'Tony Benn! Tony Benn!' I made my victory speech. Payne, the Liberal, made an angry one which was greeted with so much noise I had to quieten people down in order to allow him to be heard. Bourne, the Tory, spoke briefly.

We withdrew like boxers after a big match and went back to the Labour Club with the media in huge numbers, the police having a job to hold them back. Outside the Labour Club I spoke to the crowd again. Then I went inside and stood on a table and addressed the members. Got to bed at five, exhausted, but what an extraordinarily good result it was.

<hr>

In 1985 the privatisation programme of the Conservative Government continued with the 'Tell Sid' publicity drive to persuade individual investors to buy shares in British Gas. Tony Benn made a direct link, in a speech in December that year, between the donors to the Tory Party and the beneficiaries of the privatisations that had already taken place. Lord Stockton (Harold Macmillan) was still alive and had recently made a veiled criticism of the Tories' privatisation programme by referring to the disposal of 'the Georgian silver'.

One could not have a clearer description of the difference of opinion that divides the two sides of the House. Like a vulture, the Conservative Party is already beginning to hover around the British Gas Corporation to see what rich pickings it can make for its own people.

So far there has been no mention of the fact that many people look to gas for security of supply, high levels of maintenance and repair and high levels of safety, at a price that they can afford. During this winter, as with every other, many people will be wondering whether they will be able to pay their gas bill when it arrives later in the year. As is well known, people die every winter from hypothermia simply because they cannot afford to pay the price of fuel. Therefore to look to this industry as a way of making more profit, rather than of meeting a need, shows the real motivation behind the introduction of the Bill.

The Secretary of State was totally unconvincing. His arguments for privatisation were not valid, and he never mentioned the real reason for this measure. In 1969–70 and from 1975 to 1979 I was the sponsoring minister for the British Gas Corporation. Since the public ownership of gas there has been major investment, higher safety standards and a very good repair and maintenance record. The industry has bought British equipment, which has maintained employment, and there has been a sense of service. Successive governments have taxed the industry, but one can also tax an industry in private ownership. For example, we tax petrol. Anyone who thinks that once gas is in private ownership it will be free from a predatory Chancellor does not understand how this works. For various reasons, any Chancellor will from time to time look at ways of raising revenue, and private gas could be taxed as easily as public gas. The only difference is that gas is now being taxed for a different reason – to make it more profitable to sell it off.

I happened to be Secretary of State when North Sea gas was brought ashore. Because British Gas was a monopoly buyer, it was able to get a good price from the oil companies, because the oil companies could not play one customer off against the other. British Gas was able to say, 'If you want to sell gas in Britain, you must sell it at the price that we offer.' One reason why gas prices have been so low – in some ways too low, to make it easy for electricity and coal – is that British Gas was able to force oil companies to sell gas at a low price.

Massive investment in a new distribution network was set up and a programme to convert appliances was successfully established. The case for the common ownership of gas is unanswerable. It was not always, and only, in private ownership before nationalisation. Hon. Members might remember the phrase 'gas and water Socialism'. There was a proud municipal record of running town gas before nationalisation.

Gas is a vital national asset. Energy policy under any government is bound to take account of depletion policy. It would have been possible for British Gas, if it had so chosen and if the government had allowed it, to deplete at a massive rate and bring the gas ashore so that people converted to gas when it was cheap, only to be caught with equipment that they could not afford to use when more expensive gas came in because ours was starting to run out. Energy pricing as between gas, electricity and coal is a central part of national policy.

I should like to mention one consideration that has not come out so far, unless the Secretary of State dropped a hint. Once gas is taken out of public ownership, British Gas will be under the complete control of the Common Market Commission. I have warned the House about this before, and I am speaking from knowledge. When I was Secretary of State, it tried to argue in Brussels that the continental shelf was under the Treaty of Rome. We said that it was not and were able to enforce our will because we owned the gas fields there. The Commission wanted the pipelines to take the gas straight to Europe rather than come through our system to the continent. We were able to say, 'No, we do not accept that the continental shelf comes under the Treaty of Rome.' Privatisation will enable the Commission to enforce its will under the competition articles of the treaty. Moreover, the record of buying British equipment will dissolve, because the EEC requirement to put orders out to tender will be enforceable with a private gas corporation, whereas it was not when it was public, when we were able to have regard to the long-term security of supply of equipment.

The bill hands over North Sea gas to Common Market control by the act of privatisation. It will lead to higher prices, greater fuel poverty, lower safety, a weakening of regulation, poorer maintenance, loss of control to the EEC and reduced demand for British equipment.

The real motivation for the bill should be spelt out with absolute clarity, as the Secretary of State did not touch on it. It is to sell assets, which the government do not own, to their business friends, who will buy the assets at knockdown prices. It is to pay City institutions enormous fees to sell the assets, and to use the proceeds for a once-and-for-all tax cut to buy support at the next general election. It is important that, in addition to these technical discussions and dreams about the draft of the Queen's Speech when there is a Liberal Government – my gosh, that was interesting – we make it clear that business firms put up money to pay for Saatchi & Saatchi advertising to get a Tory Cabinet elected, knowing that a Tory Cabinet will put on the market, below their real price, assets the value of which comes from the labour of those who work in the industry concerned and from public investment. They will buy them, make a large killing and support the Tory party again. It is corruption. There is no question about it.

I have been here for thirty-five years and I have never seen a measure which so reeks of corruption as this one. We should consider the figures. British Gas is valued at £16 billion. The government have already sold

£4.7 billion of public assets and lost £1.4 billion by underpricing. That is statistically established. British Telecom shares, for example, rose 93 per cent in value before night fell, and the government lost £1.3 billion in a single day – money that would have solved the problem of inner cities, made the Archbishop of Canterbury happy, and ended the tragedy in the Broadwater Farm estate or in Brixton or in Liverpool or in Sheffield.

That money could have been used to meet needs, but it was used to pay an electoral debt incurred by the government, who gained support from business companies. If the House doubts that assertion, the figures are public. The City institutions received getting on for £300 million in fees for selling assets. That is four or five times as much as Band Aid and Live Aid raised in one year of concerts for the starving of Ethiopia. The City of London was rewarded with six times as much as the generosity of the public could provide for the starving of Ethiopia. But here is the rub. Of the City underwriters, thirty-three of the fifty-five who got the business contributed to Tory Party funds. I have some figures to prove it. Baring Brothers gave £25,000 to the Tory Party in 1983 and shared in fees of £5 million to sell off Cable & Wireless. Kleinwort Benson paid £30,000 to the Tory Party and shared in more than £5.5 million for selling British Aerospace, £190 million for selling British Telecom, more than £5 million for selling Cable & Wireless and £9 million for selling Enterprise Oil. That investment of £30,000 in Tory Party funds was pretty good. Hill Samuel paid £28,000 to the Tory Party and shared in £5.5 million of fees for the sale of Jaguar. Lazard's put in £20,000 and shared in £1.75 million for the sale of Wytch Farm. Morgan, Grenfell put in £30,000 and got a share of £3 million for the sale of Amersham International and Sealink.

When I think of the district auditor chasing councillors in Lambeth, on the grounds that they were a bit late fixing a rate, and compare that with the massive sums of money given, in effect, in return for political support to City institutions that have contributed nothing to raise the quality of service of British Gas or to provide safety for those who use it, I can only call it corruption. The public should know how it all works.

I am glad that my right hon. Friend the Member for Salford East [Mr Orme] said that an incoming Labour Government would deal with this matter. The precedents for legislation set by the Tory Party are many. I have gone through the legislation of the 1970–74 Tory Government, who took powers under the Counter-Inflation (Temporary Provisions) Act 1972 to control prices, to demand information, to amend statutes, to control profits, to vet investment and to control multinationals. They introduced the Insurance Companies (Amendment) Act 1973, which gave powers to veto directors, to inspect books, to issue directives and to define unfair practices. The fair-trading legislation gave powers which included entry and seizure. The classic case was the one-clause Rolls-Royce (Purchase) Act 1971. Through one clause, they brought Rolls-Royce into public ownership. My right hon. Friend need have no fear that he will not be sustained by Tory precedents when dealing with this abuse of public trust, which is a denial of the fiduciary responsibility to taxpayers and the public, of whom the judges are so ready to speak when they criticise Labour councillors.

There will need to be changes in the nature of public ownership. Over the years, for my sins, as Postmaster General and as an Energy Minister I have been responsible for many public corporations. There must be real accountability to Parliament. I have never believed it right for the Secretary of State of the day – I had many years' experience of this – to have no explicit authority over a chairman such as Sir Denis Rooke, but always to have to twist the chairman's arm and then not be accountable to Parliament. There should be explicit powers of direction, subject to parliamentary approval.

Secondly, we should get away from the crude patronage of appointments of board chairmen. In the United States an ambassador cannot be appointed without the approval of the Senate in committee. Parliament should have to approve the chairpersons appointed to our public corporations, so that people can give evidence about them before they are confirmed.

The third point bears a little on the question of regional boards. I was doubtful about centralisation, but it was thought necessary because of North Sea oil. Local authorities should have power over local managers of nationalised industries and be able to seek their removal if they are not sensitive to local needs.

A final precedent from the Tory Party is the Trade Union Act 1984. Many ministers have talked about the need to restore the power of union members over the unions. A minor amendment to the government's own Act would allow workers in industry to choose by ballot the boards of directors of the companies for which they work. The alteration of one word – from 'union' to 'company' – would secure a measure of power for those who have invested their lives in the gas industry, comparable with the power now supposedly enjoyed by those who have invested their money in it.

The party of which I am honoured to be a member, which still lives under the shadow of and perhaps affection for the Herbert Morrison legislation after the war, must look again at these matters. There must be accountability to Parliament. There has never been proper accountability. Parliament must be able to vet the chairmen of these great corporations. There must be accountability to elected local authorities to see that the big bosses in the public sector do not ride roughshod over local needs. Those who work in the industry must have powers over their own industrial management – based, perhaps, on the legislation introduced by the Conservatives to deal with trade-union democracy.

I have long urged those changes. When the history of all this comes to be written, for this privatisation will not last long, it may be that by breaking the Morrison mould the Government will be remembered for having paved the way to a form of common ownership which entrenches service to the public, and not the pursuit of profit which is the Government's sole interest in introducing this measure.

———————— ◄◦► ————————

At the end of 1985 official unemployment in Britain was 11.7 per cent of the workforce and, as Tony Benn commented in the following speech, 'the idea of maintaining full employment [in 1950] was a consensus point … all Conservative leaders – Churchill, Eden, right through to the noble Lord Stockton – accepted that the maintenance of full employment was one of the central points of policy'.

I should like to talk about the problems we would face if we tried to restore full employment in Britain. It has not been touched on by any government speaker because the restoration of full employment has never even been a government objective. [AN HON. MEMBER: 'Rubbish.'] It is not a government objective and no minister has ever spoken about the restoration of full employment. The problem of unemployment is a wide one and goes well beyond an economic debate. There is the tragedy of young people in Liverpool who have not worked since they left school and have no prospect of work, and the women who are doing part-time low-paid jobs and who will be affected for the worse by the change in Sunday trading.

Unemployment has an impact on the amount of money available for the public services and on the amount of money available for local government. There is also the effect of unemployment on the ethnic communities. But there is another aspect of unemployment, and that is the cost. It is very simply costed, because the Government spend £7.5 billion a year on unemployment pay. The loss of taxation and National Insurance as a result of four million unemployed is another £12.5 billion. That is £20 billion basic, but then there is a loss of production by the people who are unemployed.

If we take it as a reasonable assumption that people in work could have at least 80 per cent of their production matched by those out of work, we are talking about another £52 billion of production, if we had full employment. With so much suffering and so much cost, why have this government abandoned the objective of full employment?

When I first came into the House thirty-five years ago this month, the idea of maintaining full employment was a consensus point. Harold Macmillan has now appeared in the House of Lords commenting again, but of course all Conservative leaders – Churchill, Eden, right through to the noble Lord – accepted that the maintenance of full employment was one of the central points of policy. It is fair to say that the policies pursued by the consensus governments that followed one another did not succeed. That is why I do not listen with enthusiasm to Harold Macmillan, while others do.

That was the objective, and now that objective has been dropped. The fact that it has been dropped is not an accident. I have never accepted the idea of what is sometimes called Thatcherism. I do not believe that it is about monetarism, and I do not believe that political decisions are taken by going into a room with a cold towel round one's head and looking at a calculator to find out what the Public Sector Borrowing Requirement will be. After looking at the experience of the consensus years, the government decided that they needed the dole to discipline the workforce. That is what it is about.

The hon. Member for Bury North [Mr Burt] said how happy people are and that they are all at one. What has happened is that the fear of unemployment has given management a power that it has not had since the 1920s or Victorian times.

Unemployment performs vital economic functions. It keeps wages down. If a worker goes to his employer and says, 'I cannot live on the money', the employer will say that there are four million people on the dole who will be happy to do the job. For the same reason, unemployment weakens the unions. It undermines the public services, which are costly. The government do not want to finance them. Unemployment justifies rate-capping and, of course, it boosts profits. If wages are kept down, marvellous profit figures can be produced, and it is the profit figures that make the Cabinet confident, because they do not intend to go back to full employment and do not believe in doing so.

To restore full employment, it would be necessary, with four million unemployed and a five-year Parliament, to create one million new jobs a year. That is what it would take to get back to what was the consensus of all parties in Parliament for forty years.

I take up the point made by my hon. Friend the Member for Newham North-East [Mr Leighton]. Twice in my lifetime we have created one million new jobs a year, all funded by public expenditure. The first time was from 1938 to 1942. It was public expenditure on rearmament at the end of the 1930s that gave us one million new jobs a year. That was when the PSBR was 27 per cent of the national output – ten times what it is today. If people are taken off the dole, put into armaments factories and taxed on their earnings, the project finances itself. It was done by very strong central direction and by public expenditure.

I do not need to stress to the House that rearmament was not done by private expenditure. Granny did not buy a Bren gun, mother did not have a tank, and father did not buy a Spitfire with an A-registration. It was all done by the government. People say that government cannot create jobs. Of course they can, if they wish to do so.

The second example was from 1945 to 1948, when we brought three million service men out of the armed forces and put them back to work. It was the biggest example of defence conversion that there has ever been. Compared with it, the problems of defence conversion that an incoming Labour Government would face would be simple. In Bristol, my old constituency, the Bristol Aeroplane Company, as it used to be, stopped sending out trucks with Blenheim bombers and a few months later it was producing prefabricated houses. That was done by having a central control over the economy. The powers were there and the objective was clear. The powers were used. If we want to restore full employment, it will not be done by tinkering about with the PSBR.

I did not hear the whole of the speech of the right hon. Member for Glasgow Hillhead [Mr Jenkins], but anyone who thinks that joining the European monetary system and going back to an incomes policy will get us back to full employment is absolutely wrong, because those actions are simply tinkering on the margin. If we want to get back to full employment – the objective that we should set ourselves in Britain, for a range of social, political and economic reasons – we shall have to do more than that. We must re-equip and re-establish British manufacturing industry by direct methods. It is no good speaking about industry as if it is an optional extra, assuming that if it loses it can be closed down, as if manufacturing is like white side-walled tyres – one has it if one can afford it. We have got to have industry.

One of the reasons why the Japanese are so successful is that they look ahead for ten or twenty years. Any sensible planning of a modern society would include the planning of investment in high-technology industries and in the maintenance of what are now called the smokestack industries, mainly to justify closing them.

Next, we would have to refurbish and develop the infrastructure. I am often amazed when I see industrialists, whose whole market depends on public expenditure, calling for cuts in public expenditure. Hon. Members will know the old joke in the construction industry that sewage is their bread and butter. When sewers are renewed and when bridges are built, there are jobs for the construction industry, and we need a modern infrastructure, but that would involve public expenditure.

Next, we would have to expand the public services. If it is said that now that we have the microchip there is no demand, I could take any Member of this House, as other hon. Members could, to hundreds of houses where there are old people. In the modern jargon, they are now called the psycho-geriatrics. They are simply a bit old and confused. They need homes to live in; they need twenty-four-hours-a-day care. To meet their needs would create jobs. We need day centres. We need crèches so that women can be released to go to work or to college. No one can persuade me that Britain is not full of things that need to be done. Just as rearmament brought us back to full employment, so the expansion of the public services can bring us back to full employment.

If technology allows us to achieve the necessary national output without seven days a week of back-breaking work, let us have earlier retirement and a shorter working week. Let us raise the school-leaving age, and enable adults to go in and out of education. If we wish to do those things, we shall have to plan our trade, for if we reflate the economy when we have not a manufacturing base, we shall be flooded not with imports of the raw materials or engineering products which will be needed, but with consumer products.

If people had to wait a little longer for a Honda, but could get a hip operation a bit sooner, what would be wrong with that? That is the sort of priority we would have to set. Unemployment is a form of import control. An unemployed person cannot afford a Japanese video, French wine or American tobacco. The government have import controls, but they apply only to the unemployed, the low-paid and the people living on supplementary benefits.

We would have to stop the export of capital. Since the government came to power, for every family of four, £4,300 has left Britain. The Chancellor of the Exchequer says that we must tighten our belts because that is the way to solve the problem. But if a worker tightens his belt, the employer sends the money to South Africa, where the wages are lower still, because Botha's police will not allow the unions to organise. The export of capital could not continue if we wished to solve the unemployment problem.

We would also have to ease the arms burden. I have already mentioned Japan, but people do not often talk openly of the fact that the Japanese spend only 1 per cent of a much bigger national income on defence. We spend 6 per cent. Why are the shops in Britain full of Japanese videos, cameras and motorcycles? It is because that is what the Japanese produce. Our government's hopes are based on tourism and selling battlefield communications systems to the Americans. We have abandoned the serious intent of being a major manufacturing nation. That policy would have to change.

The Secretary of State for Defence comes to every household every week and takes £24 off a family of four to finance the defence burden.

We would have to deal with the Treaty of Rome. We could not solve any of the problems under a constitution which makes it illegal to intervene with market forces.

We would have to have a major expansion of public responsibility and control over our economy.

I do not believe that anything less than the measures I have outlined would bring us anywhere near to the achievement of full employment. The government do not want it. The wets could not get it, although they tried. The SDP–Liberal Alliance thinks that if we squeeze the wages in Whitehall, join the European monetary system and have a federal Europe, full employment will come automatically.

The Mitterrand dash for growth came a cropper because he did not really deal with the power structure. His economy zoomed up and fell flat. Mitterrand's policy failed because, apart from anything else, he could not escape from the Treaty of Rome. The Treaty of Rome and the way in which it operated brought down the French economy.

To achieve full employment we need fundamental changes in our policy and in our thinking. If this House is to be a forum for the nation, one of its functions is to tell the people outside that we cannot have full employment simply by tinkering with the economy. If we want full employment again, we have to set the objective and take the powers to bring it about. We must have the courage to implement it. That is what the choice will be when the general election comes. It will not be much influenced by whether there are a few tax cuts, purchased by selling off public assets. The choice will be a basic one. I have a feeling that, after their experience with this government, the British people will be ready to take it.

*Spycatcher: The Candid Autobiography of a Senior Intelligence Officer,
written by Peter Wright (of MI5) and Paul Greengrass and published
in Australia in 1985, had been banned from the UK because of the
sensitive nature of some of its revelations. However, it was legally
available in Scotland and elsewhere, and attempts by the government
through the courts to prevent publication of any extracts were ineffective
and widely ridiculed. In July 1987 the case became absurd when the
Law Lords again imposed a ban on the book, and Tony Benn decided to
read extracts from it in public in London on 2 August, surrounded by
journalists with tape recorders and TV cameras, who were not allowed
to report his words. This was the essence of his speech.*

It was here in Hyde Park that free speech was established over
a hundred years ago and we are meeting today in an attempt to
prevent ministers and judges destroying our inherent, inalienable
and democratic rights.

Mr Peter Wright has alleged in his book *Spycatcher* that certain public
servants, working for the security services, have broken the law many
times, and have even attempted to subvert an elected government in
which I, along with others, served as a Cabinet minister. But instead
of investigating these allegations, the Attorney General has applied
for, and won from the judges, injunctions to prevent these reports of
alleged illegalities from being published at all, and even the House of
Commons has been inhibited from debating the issues on the grounds
that they were *sub judice*.

Let me quote now from the book itself. On page 31 Mr Wright
alleges: 'We did have fun. For five years we bugged and burgled our
way across London at the State's behest, while pompous bowler-hatted
civil servants in Whitehall pretended to look the other way.'

On page 60 Mr Wright alleges: 'At the beginning of the Suez crisis MI6 developed a plan through the London station, to assassinate Nasser using nerve gas. Eden initially gave his approval to this operation.'

... Writing of the end of the Heath Government, Mr Wright alleges:

> As events moved to their political climax in early 1974,
> with the election of the minority Labour government,
> MI5 was sitting on information which if leaked would
> undoubtedly have caused a political scandal of incalculable
> consequences. The news that the Prime Minister was
> himself being investigated would at the least have led to his
> resignation. The point was not lost on some MI5 officers.

... Those, then, are just a few of the quotations from Mr Wright's book, in which he makes a large number of very serious allegations.

If any of them are true, MI5 officers were incited to break the law, have broken the law, did attempt – with CIA help – to destroy an elected government, and any responsible Prime Minister should have instructed the police to investigate, with a view to prosecution, and the courts should have convicted and sentenced those found guilty. The charge which the Prime Minister, the Lord Chancellor, the Law Officers, the police have to face is that they have betrayed their public trust, and the judges who have upheld them are in clear breach of Article One of the Bill of Rights of 1689. For if ministers can arbitrarily suspend the law and claim that issues of confidentiality, or national security, justify a ban on publication, and if the judges issue an injunction, there could be no limit to the suppression of information which might embarrass any government.

I have come here today, first as a citizen, but also as an elected Member of Parliament, a Privy Councillor and a member of the

Committee of Privileges of the House of Commons, to warn that we cannot, and should not, accept this restriction on our liberty.

———————— ‹◊› ————————

Sunday 31 December 1989

A tumultuous decade and a dramatic year have ended.

World politics in 1989 were earth-shattering. In Poland, Lech Walesa came to power and emerged as a real right-wing, Thatcherite, Catholic nationalist for whom I have very little sympathy. He came to Britain saying he was going to offer cheap Polish labour to British investors, and told the CBI he wanted profit to play a larger part. Then there were demonstrations in Prague, which were put down by force and led to the total overthrow of the Czech regime and a new government. Hungary developed in a similar way. Then the Berlin Wall came down after tremendous outpourings of public feeling, the East and West German governments came together, and there was talk of German reunification. All this was accepted by Gorbachev, who is still desperately trying to make a go of his reforms in Russia, but there are problems in Armenia and the Baltic States, and the economic situation is terribly difficult. The Tories argued that this had all come about due to the fact that we had nuclear weapons, but people didn't really believe it any more.

———————— ‹◊› ————————

CHAPTER FIVE

Diarist

In 1992 the Labour leader, Neil Kinnock, having lost a second general election, resigned as leader and was succeeded by John Smith. Within two years Smith was dead and was soon written out of Labour's history. The reforms of the Party, which had been spearheaded by left groups such as the Campaign for Labour Party Democracy, were replaced by the New Labour project. As well as continuing to be an active constituency MP for Chesterfield (holding a series of 'Chesterfield socialist conferences'), Tony Benn had established himself by the mid-1990s as a chronicler of the twentieth century through his immense archives and his diaries (which eventually spanned the years 1940–2012). For a while successive students (among whom were Edward Miliband, Simon Fletcher and Andrew Hood) were engaged in his basement office in cataloguing his papers. Andrew co-authored a book with Tony during this period, calling for a new constitution for Britain. The 'Balkan Wars' also revived Tony's anti-war campaigning role, at times setting him against other figures on the left.

By 1993 the Treaty of Maastricht had turned the European Community into a union, and the UK had ignominiously left the Exchange Rate Mechanism (intended as a precursor to joining the euro). The bitterness of these measures took its toll on John Major and his party; the Labour Party, though ostensibly united on the EU, also had a number of dissenters.

The Major government of 1992–7 was also beset by a series of 'sleaze' allegations, of which the Neil Hamilton case was one of the more notorious, centring on his financial relationship with Mohammed Al Fayed. The cases resulted in the establishment of the Committee on Standards in Public Life, under which its second chairman, Sir Patrick Neill, investigated the Hamilton case. Going against the tide of parliamentary consensus and forensically examining the role of the Commons in self-regulation of its Members, Tony Benn refused to support Hamilton's recommended expulsion from the Commons unless by the voters.

Tuesday 4 August 1992

Up very early and the Teabags began gathering at home for a working week at Stansgate: we picked up two Transit trucks with boxes of archives and drove to Essex in about two and a half hours.

There were notes from Caroline on domestic arrangements and from Ruth on the archival tasks, and I have given everyone a Teabag T-shirt. We had a lovely meal.

There was a conducted tour and late in the evening we talked about the book. This is the book on the constitution that we are supposed to be writing, and so we worked out whether we could write something that was really different, to break out of the total stagnation of British politics.

Wednesday 5 August

A very early start. The work began in earnest on the archives.

It's the first proper holiday I have had for ages. I'm finding it exhausting – all the physical work of lifting and humping – but tremendously useful.

Thursday 6 August

I was out in the garden in one of the buildings, sorting out my papers and archives, and somebody called out to say I had a phone call from King Hussein of Jordan. So I ran in and picked up the phone and he said, 'Sir, this is King Hussein speaking.' I can never recover from the fact that he always calls everyone sir.

I said, 'I am awfully sorry, I was in the garden.'

'What a good place to be,' he said. 'I wanted to thank you very much for your message' – because I had sent him a copy of my letter to the Secretary General of the UN about a visit to Baghdad. 'I agree strongly with the line you take. It's difficult, people don't take much notice of us.'

'Would I be right in saying that the Gulf War had really played some part in stimulating fundamentalism in Egypt and Algeria?'

'Oh yes, certainly,' he said.

I asked him about the Secretary General of the UN and he said that he was taking a more independent line and balancing the various crises: Somalia, Iraq and the situation in the Balkans, Yugoslavia.

I wouldn't be human if I didn't admit that I was much flattered that the King rang me personally.

———◦———

I have no brief for Mr Hamilton. What he did was utterly disreputable, so I have no complaint about what was said about him, but one thought occurs to me: did he break the law? I say that because the one thing that the House of Commons has totally failed to deal with throughout this matter is its own failure to lay down standards for all Members of

Parliament. That is the issue that I wish the Committee [on Standards and Privileges] had found time to consider.

What Mr Hamilton did may, or may not, be widespread; I do not want to go into that. It may or may not extend to all parties; I do not want to go into that. Certainly the sale of peerages has been known. It is a problem that has to be viewed in a very broad context. However, the whole debate has been overtaken by a wider question – not just cash for questions, but cash for politics. On what condition should money be made available for political action, either by an individual or by others?

We have heard all the arguments about self-regulation. Self-regulation means, in effect, that we decide on an arbitrary basis, instead of laying down the law as to what should or should not be acceptable and leaving judges to determine it. If Parliament passes a law saying what is and is not acceptable, that is self-regulation, but the determination falls to the judges, not to the House. There was always a problem with this in election cases which were transmitted to an election court instead of an election committee. A majority party always has a sort of interest in protecting its own members, which is why election cases are no longer handled in that way.

I am not in favour of Sir Patrick Neill being the man responsible for making recommendations of this kind. It is for the House to decide, on a considered judgement based on draft legislation. I shall take only a minute or two to try to identify what the law could have been that could have prevented this happening.

Just as a corrupt practice is defined in an election, so a corrupt practice should be defined for a Member of Parliament. What the House determined to do in legislation would be a matter for it to decide, but if someone were charged with a corrupt practice as a Member of Parliament, the matter could go to a court to determine.

The person concerned would be able to present his case.

I have committed every known offence. I have been thrown out by an election court, but at least I had the opportunity to present my case, which I was not allowed to do to the Privileges Committee. I spoke for a week, which is the longest speech I have ever made in my life, the House will be glad to hear. At the end, two judges said that I was disqualified, as I had committed an even more serious offence –my blood had gone blue.

Has anyone ever looked at the list of disqualifications? It is as long as your arm, as we are always adding to it. Certain relationships should be disqualifying relationships. If it turned out that a Member of Parliament was working for Al Fayed or someone else and that was listed as a disqualifying office, that Member would be out, but it would be determined by law and not by the arbitrary proceedings of a secret committee that operated without protection for those who were charged.

I should like to finish. I know that many hon. Members wish to speak, and I think my hon. Friend will agree that I have a long interest in this matter.

There must be transparency. The complaint about Mr Hamilton is straightforward. If it had been known what he was up to, he would have been dealt with years ago. Indeed, the real remedy for Mr Hamilton was his electorate, who dealt with him. That is the proper way to deal with people who have not done anything illegal but who have done something unacceptable.

I have never believed that the House had the right to throw out Members – none of us is here because the House wanted us, but we are here because our electors sent us here. The proper remedy for inappropriate behaviour is the electorate, and the proper remedy for illegal behaviour is the courts. Somehow, in the middle of all this, my right hon. Friend the Member for Ashton-under-Lyne [Mr Sheldon], a distinguished body of people, and a Commissioner hanging around to help him, have fallen between two stools.

I shall outline briefly what I think should be done. There should be a public register of gifts from individuals and organisations. Organisations and companies should have a ballot before they give money, just as trade unions do. Why should a company be able to give money without consulting shareholders, when trade unions have to have a ballot? Companies should register any gifts and services that they offer to parties and to individuals.

Similarly, individuals and parties should be required to register the gifts and services that they have received – the amount and the recipient. I have said this before, but I repeat it now – this information should appear on the ballot paper. Voters should know the interests of candidates. The electorate are the proper remedy for inappropriate behaviour.

If the people of Tatton, or anywhere else, want to vote for someone engaged in something that is not illegal, and that person has listed all his relationships, it is up to them to decide whether they want him. If it says on the ballot paper that the candidate is a director of fifteen companies or is sponsored by the Transport and General Workers' Union, they will decide whether or not they want him. We are really discussing the rights of the electors, not the rights of Parliament. There should also be a cap on election law.

I am broadening the argument a little, but it is obvious in the light of what has happened recently that the question of cash for politics is more interesting and relevant than the issue of cash for questions.

It is not a matter of trust – I have never been inclined in my life to distrust people – but a question of law and responsibility. As a member of the Labour Party, I would like to know who gives money to the Labour Party, what they have given and when they gave it. That does not require legislation, but is a matter for me as a member of the Labour Party. The Shadow Leader of the House said that Mr Hamilton would not be on another Conservative candidates list, and that is a matter for the Conservative Party.

We are dealing here with transparency and the law. If we had had a combination of a clear statement of the law, judges to determine whether the law had been broken and transparency in financial relations, the Hamilton case would never have occurred. I regret that my right hon. Friend the Chairman of the Committee, whom I deeply admire, has moved his report. I shall not vote against it, of course, but I cannot support what I regard as a classic failure by the House of Commons to do its proper job – to lay down the proper and improper things that a Member of Parliament can do.

***

Saturday 23 January 1993

I went to Worcester today to speak for the Worcester Miners' support group. It was a long boring journey via Oxford. On the train I had a friendly argument with the people on board, because the train from London to Oxford had No Smoking compartments. I think that's intolerable. So I said to the guard, 'I'm going to light my pipe.'

'Oh no you're not,' he said with a friendly smile. 'Come and smoke in my compartment.'

So he took me to the driver's cabin and we had a chat. I do feel somebody's got to take a stand on behalf of smokers. You should take no notice whatever of No Smoking notices unless somebody asks you not to smoke; and if they do, then you put out your pipe or cigarette immediately. I think that's the principle that should be established.

Came back on the last train; was a bit more courageous. With my fingernails I removed the No Smoking notice from the window and just sat there and smoked my pipe. The guard came by and didn't say a word.

Sunday 19 February 1995

I don't want to retire from politics, but I don't just want to be the same old Tony Benn. I don't want, either, to make the same mistake of the so-called democratic left who began coming to terms with Thatcherism and the new times. That would be a corruption and I'm simply not going to do that.

I'd like to throw a light on the future, the next century; what can we reasonably expect; how will it all develop: the environment, animal welfare, housing, local government, democracy, Europe? I'm a bit nervous that if I tried to do it I wouldn't have the intellectual capacity to produce anything any good. That's why I tend to stay in the old grooves.

I was thinking the other day that if Clem Attlee and Ernie Bevin were still in Parliament at the age of 110, and were still asking questions and writing Early Day Motions and trying to chip into debates, people would say, 'For God's sake, Clem and Ernie, you've had your time – move over!' I've got to learn to cope with old age.

Wednesday 8 March 1995

I went off to the House of Commons with my camera to meet up with Abercrombie Primary school from Chesterfield. It is a simply lovely school. The kids are bright as anything. There was a little boy called Michael who was the cleverest of all. When the guide asked them about the English Civil War, Michael said, 'It was a war between the Roundheads and the Vauxhalls.' He'd muddled up, of course, the Vauxhall Cavalier with the Cavaliers. It was so sweet.

We went into a committee room and I asked them about hunting, and the majority were against it.

Then they said, 'Can we have a debate?' I asked, 'What do you want to debate?' 'Well,' they said, 'are you in favour of violent sport, like boxing?' A boy got up and said, 'I think boxing's a good idea.' A girl got up and said, 'You could get damaged.' Somebody else said, 'You should have more padding.' Another girl said, 'Yes, but that doesn't always help.' It was a marvellous debate and in the end we had a vote – it was 19–7 for the abolition of boxing!

———————◦►———————

Gordon Brown's famous criteria that had to be met before Britain would join the euro under a Labour Government were the subject of a debate in June 1998. It gave Tony Benn another opportunity to appraise the Europe issue and, in typically striking language, he warned, 'We are tonight consenting to an act of unilateral economic, industrial and financial disarmament.' In the event, the criteria were never (and perhaps never intended to be) met and Britain has remained outside the Eurozone to date.

I have not participated in the debate on Europe since the election [of 1997], because my view on the matter is known: I voted against the Maastricht Treaty, and I am opposed to the single currency.

The reason I speak in this debate is that it is held against the background of a clear government statement of intent to join the single currency, when the conditions are appropriate. The convergence report is a progress report – the government ask us, not only to note, but to approve the progress they are making towards entry into the single currency when the referendum has occurred. We are told that that will be after the next election, but, if Rupert Murdoch alters his view, it might come earlier.

Two passages in the report are of importance, not just in a debate of this kind in the House, but to many people outside. On page 6 the report refers to Denmark, Spain, Ireland, the Netherlands, Portugal, Finland and the United Kingdom. It says: 'These Member States need to exercise firm control over domestic price pressures with regard to, inter alia, wage and unit labour costs. Support is also required from fiscal policies, which need to react flexibly to the domestic price environment.'

If I were a nurse whose pay claim had been phased, I would ask why. If a nurse asked me that question, I would reply, 'The answer is in this book, because it is a requirement that these controls be exercised in order to equip us for the single currency.' I come from Derbyshire, where we are rate-capped, and if, in Derbyshire, people ask me, 'Why is Derbyshire, which suffered so much under the previous government, being rate-capped?' I would answer, 'Because of page 6 of the convergence report.'

We must relate these arguments to real life. We cannot speak as though we were amateur economists; we must relate them to the real lives of those we represent. The reality is that the framework, set by the European Monetary Institute and adopted by the government, is forcing a squeeze on people, who will suffer as a result.

My second point – I do not want to take too long – relates to the independence of national central banks. On page 12 the report says clearly that a list of practices by governments or parliaments are incompatible with the Treaty and/or the Statute if they endanger institutional independence – that is, from governments or parliaments. So here, tonight, we are being asked to accept that we have no right in the following areas. We have no right to give instructions to central banks or their decision-making bodies, not just on interest rates, but on anything that they do. Eddie George, Bank of England Governor, is free – protected by the treaty from any pressures that may be put on him by the government elected overwhelmingly by the people in May 1997.

Indeed, it would be incompatible with the treaty to 'approve, suspend, annul or defer decisions of national central banks; or to censor a national central bank's decisions on legal grounds'. Whatever the legislation might be, the courts would not be allowed to take action that would hamper the independence of the central banks. Indeed, we cannot 'participate in the decision-making bodies of a national central bank with a right to vote'. Therefore, if the Chancellor appoints people to the Monetary Policy Committee and they vote on a matter, they are in breach of the Maastricht Treaty.

Finally, third parties could not be 'consulted (ex ante)' – in advance – on any national central bank decision. Tonight not only are we approving a policy – which is causing hardship to many people because of the restriction on public expenditure, and because, as has been said, the currency valuation affects jobs – but we are being asked to approve an abandonment of our right ever to do anything in those areas that might relieve those pressures.

I believe that my right hon. Friend, Mr Llew Smith (Blaenau Gwent) is right to say that we would not have the rights, as a Parliament, to instruct the European Central Bank on issues such as unemployment, but surely it goes further. Not only would we not have the right, but it would be positively illegal if we tried to influence the European Central Bank on issues such as unemployment, low pay and poverty. If that is the case – if Parliament no longer controls economic policy-making – surely, at elections, the people will then find that the people they can vote for are not the people who take the decisions. The people they want to have an opportunity to vote for – the bankers – will be taking the decisions. Surely that makes a mockery of parliamentary democracy.

I object to these arrangements, not as a British person, but as a European, because they destroy democracy in Germany and France, too. For example, the German people will be unable to influence the decision of their bankers. My hon. Friend referred to the limitation on our opportunity, as a nation, to try to influence the European Central Bank, but it applies also to attempts to influence our own bank.

To summarise, we are tonight consenting to an act of unilateral economic, industrial and financial disarmament. From now on we are saying to our electors – who are, after all, the people who have sent us here and can remove us, because we are still candidates – 'You can remove us next time, but you will never be able to change the policies that may lead you to want to remove us.'

That is a big question. It is something that we do not often discuss and, if we do, sometimes in the heat of the day and in argument we get strong and personal, because it is a matter which cuts across political allegiances. It is a European, and a democratic, question.

We are all, inevitably, influenced by our own experience. The earliest election that I remember was that in 1931, when the conflicts within the Labour Cabinet on whether the gold standard should apply led to the fall of that government. My father lost his seat in that election. He had the unhappy experience of fighting Aberdeen, whose electors were cautious when the Post Office scare appeared, Aberdonians being known for their caution.

In the 1930s I remember vividly Hitler coming to power when there were five million or six million unemployed in Germany. I bought *Mein Kampf* when I was eleven. I have it on my shelf at home. Unemployment leads to despair, and despair destroys democracy, just as political impotence destroys democracy. If, when we vote, we cannot change anything, that destroys democracy. There are now fifteen million unemployed in the European Union. I am not saying that what happened in the 1930s will return, but we are dealing with big questions.

We are dealing with the question of whether it is legitimate in countries that boast of democracy for the electors to elect a government and a parliament that can influence the form of their own lives. It applies throughout the EU. This is not a British objection – I would feel just as strongly if I were a Frenchman, a Spaniard, a Greek or from any other country.

We shall have more of this when we come to the debates on the single currency, but it is important to put down a marker now, before we go along quietly approving things which are already taking place, beginning with the independence of the Bank of England, and denying those who sent us here the rights that they are entitled to expect when they cast their vote. For those reasons, I shall not be able to support the motion tonight. It runs counter to my deepest convictions, and that is a view that I hope people will understand, even if they do not agree with it.

Proportional representation as a voting system divides the Conservative and Labour Parties and has been a consideration in party negotiations for at least 100 years. Both parties are inclined to entertain the idea when in opposition and forget about it when they are in office. Tony was always vehemently opposed to PR. The context of the debate in November 1998 was Roy Jenkins's report on whether a form of PR could be adopted for the British electoral system. Nothing came of it!

This is an important debate, whatever view we take, because we are discussing the basis of our authority. I will have been here forty-eight years at the end of the month, and it seems to me that people want a representative when they vote. The idea that every Liberal or Labour voter supports every item of Liberal or Labour Party policy is absolute nonsense. People want to be represented. Introducing proportionality completely destroys the idea of representation.

When we discussed the subject in the Labour Party's National Executive a few years ago, when Neil Kinnock was leader, I said to Neil that I had a feeling that if we had a party list system, my hon. Friend the Member for Bolsover [Mr Skinner] and I would be at the bottom of the list. He laughed, but in a funny sort of way. That is the direction in which politics is going.

No doubt all hon. Members will go to their constituencies this weekend. Every person whom we meet in our constituencies is our employer – the bus driver, the street sweeper, the home help, the policeman – and has the power to remove us. Our constituents expect to be represented. They decide whether they agree with our views and whether we have done a decent job.

Any element of proportionality, which destroys that link, could lead to people being governed by a government whom nobody had voted for, because nobody would know the basis of the coalition on polling day. At least the coalitions of the parties are transparent: people can see them developing and know what they are voting for and what their own Member thinks.

I do not intend to waste much time on the Jenkins report because, candidly, I do not think that it has a cat in hell's chance of succeeding. The idea that the Parliamentary Labour Party would go through the Lobby to destroy fifty of its own Members, to redraw all the constituencies and to introduce a new group of piggyback Members is ludicrous. I heard it said by one cynic that the Labour Party is so loyal that, if chimney boys were brought back in the name of modernisation, we would all go through the Lobby; but turkeys do not vote for Christmas. I do not honestly think that this is a serious plan.

The real issue is one that Jenkins neither considered, nor was asked to consider, the power that people have over the government of their country. This is the beginning of a debate about democracy generally. Unlike almost every other country, we have no vote over the Head of State. We have no vote over the second Chamber. If my right hon. Friend the Prime Minister reintroduces Edward I's method of appointing peers – when peers began in 1295, they were not hereditary – we will be modernising ourselves back to the feudal period. There will be absolutely no popular control.

The House of Commons has very limited power. After all, the Prime Minister derives his legislative majority from the people, but most of his executive power from the Crown. That is why the Prime Minister has put a spin-doctor into Buckingham Palace. If the Crown is not popular, the Prime Minister might lose the power to appoint bishops, judges, commissioners, peers, and so on. That is how the system works.

It amazes me that the British people put up with that system. What is it about our training and breeding that makes us think that we are not fit to elect the second Chamber or the Head of State? Jenkins does not deal with that, because he is an Asquithian Liberal. We have to be very careful.

People ask whether the proposals would lead to a coalition; but they are all about getting a coalition. Those who advocate the proposals favour a coalition. I do not want to be too political in a debate of this character, but it is worth noting that there is a big Labour majority and the Leader of the Liberal Party is on a Cabinet Committee, but I am not. I met him voting against the lone-parents provisions last December. I was threatened with disciplinary action, but he knew that he would be at the Cabinet Committee the next day. There is already a broad perspective of views. For example, the right hon. Member for Henley [Mr Heseltine], the former Deputy Prime Minister, has been given a job and the former Chancellor has been given a job. The former chairman of the Conservative Party is in Northern Ireland, clearing up the RUC, and David Mellor is in charge of football. When we talk about inclusiveness, I just wish some of us were part of it.

In future, unless we are clear about stopping it, all candidates will be vetted by the party machines. That is not about the power of the Prime Minister, but the power of the party leader. All the European candidates have been vetted and put on a list, as have all the Scottish candidates. My hon. Friend the Member for Falkirk West [Mr Canavan] was left off, because he was thought less suitable to be a Scottish candidate, although the hon. Member for Leominster [Mr Temple-Morris] has suddenly given the Labour voters there a Member of Parliament by changing sides. Candidates for the Welsh Assembly will also be vetted. So the language of devolution is accompanied by the centralisation of power.

I do not wish to overdo the point, but as a minister I visited the Soviet Union and Brussels many times. In the Soviet Union we used to meet the Central Committee, which had not been elected. We met the Commissars, and they had not been elected. I went to Brussels and met representatives of the Central Bank, and that had not been elected. I met the Commissioners, and they had not been elected. The truth is that capitalism and communism have one thing in common – they do not want the people to have a choice of system, only a choice of management. That is the problem that we face. I have not heard anybody suggest that it would be a good idea for the Governor of the Bank of England to be elected, even by first-past-the-post, and he has more power than any of us here. He is appointed, so he depends, like the bishops and the judges, on patronage.

We must face the problem that government now is less about representation and more about management. I get my fax from the party headquarters every morning, with quotations already attributed to me – 'Mr Tony Benn welcomes compulsory homework for pensioners', or whatever it is, and I am supposed to put it back in the fax machine to send to the *Derbyshire Times*. I feel less and less like a representative and more and more like an Avon lady, who is told what to say when she knocks at the door. If the Liberals had joined the right end of the Labour Party, we might have had a progressive party, but the trouble is that they joined the wrong end of the Labour Party. I will not go into that now.

Direct representation is the delicate thread that links the people with their government and the basis of it is that they elect a man or woman they know, can argue with and can get rid of. Do not think that minorities remain minorities for ever. After all, ten years ago the environmentalists were bearded weirdos, but it will not be long before Swampy (the Ecowarrior) is in the House of Lords. The Dunblane massacre led to the previous government changing their policy, and apartheid ended by popular pressure. Democracy is not what somebody does to us if we vote for them, but what we do where we live and work, and Parliament then gets the message. After forty-eight years here, I can say that Parliament usually gets the message last. We must listen to the people and not try to impose on them a pattern that will provide a permanent coalition and remove real choice from the electors.

—◦—

All 306 British soldiers who were executed during the First World for desertion or cowardice were the subject of a passionately fought campaign by Andrew Mackinlay and others to secure them a posthumous pardon from successive Labour Defence Ministers. In 2006 the campaign was finally successful.

May I join in thanking the Secretary of State – and particularly my hon. Friend the Member for Thurrock [Mr Mackinlay] – for the very sensitive and imaginative way in which he has dealt with the matter? However, are we not speaking about a little bit more than the victims of war? Are we not speaking about the victims of the law, passed by Parliament, that conscripted young men and women who did not wish to fight and told them – under the then military code – 'If you do not kill under orders, we will execute you'? They were victims of Parliament and of war, although the two were interconnected in that case. May I ask him also to recognise that the real victims today – for those who were shot have gone – are the families who have the anguish of knowing that their fathers, grandfathers, uncles and great-uncles died as convicted of cowardice?

In the light of Archbishop Tutu's institution of a Truth and Reconciliation Commission to bring out the truth and allow the past to rest in peace, could not the word 'pardon' be used to recognise that – for the benefit of the families – those people really were not guilty of the military offence for which they were sentenced to death? I ask the Secretary of State to consider that proposal in the light of the families who suffer, still to this day, for what happened to those who went before.

—◦—

Tuesday 7 September 1999

After lunch I had a phone call saying Alan Clark, the local MP for Kensington and Chelsea, had died. Some of the things he said were outrageous, but on the Balkan War he and I were totally opposed to it and he spoke out very strongly.

He was a serious historian; his study of one of the disastrous battles of the First World War, called 'The Donkeys', is very famous. He was a diarist of course, although his diaries didn't say much about politics; less well known is the fact that he was a vegetarian, against hunting and, as a minister, tried to stop the import of fur from animals that had been trapped, though that policy was vetoed by the Tory Government because the Canadians depended on it.

He was very kindly. I've never forgotten the speech he gave at Bob Cryer's memorial meeting.

Wednesday 13 February 2002

Had a terrible problem with my electricity supply. London Electricity came to cut me off saying I'd transferred to npower. I said I hadn't. I rang npower, but they didn't know anything about it. I rang London Electricity; they gave me a reference number. I rang npower again; they said it was a mistake. I rang London Electricity back and they said this happens two or three times a day in London. What an outrage it is! The lights went off later in the day. I don't know why, but all the lights in the area went off.

—◦—

Kosovo 19 April 1999

The collapse of Yugoslavia and the ensuing Balkan wars meant that in 1998–9 NATO became involved in Kosovo with strong support given by the British government under Tony Blair.

If ever there were a case that justified the House of Commons, it is today's debate. There is disagreement – I shall try to vote against the war tonight – so we should be clear about what we agree on.

There are no apologists for Milosevic in the House. Nobody here could conceive of endorsing, supporting or accepting ethnic cleansing. There are people who are concerned about not only the refugees in Kosovo, but the 300,000 Serb refugees from Krajina, who are now being bombed in their refuge in Yugoslavia, and the Serbs who have left Kosovo because of the Kosovo Liberation Army. The Foreign Secretary told us in January that the KLA had killed more Serbs than the Serbs had Albanians.

The argument is not even about force. I favour the use of force, but not by NATO. I want to be specific and clear about that. As I have said in earlier debates, I am of a generation for whom the United Nations charter was the great hope of the world. The charter said clearly that force could be used, but only by the Security Council. When NATO was formed, article 1 of its constitution – I looked it up to remind myself of its words – said that its members 'shall refrain in their international relations from the threat or use of force ... in any ... manner inconsistent with the Purposes of the United Nations'.

NATO is breaking its own constitution. I shall turn in a moment to what hope NATO might have of achieving anything. The House is, if I may say so, ill informed by the media and the government.

The annex of the Rambouillet Agreement says that NATO personnel would be permitted to enter into Yugoslavia from any border – Bosnia, Croatia, Hungary, Macedonia – with machinery, arms ammunition and men. Furthermore they have to be given all assistance from the military and civilian authorities throughout Yugoslavia, and would be able to leave their arms in Yugoslav Army depots, or where they so choose. That was not an agreement; it was an ultimatum. It said to the Serbs, 'If you don't accept this, we will bomb you.'

What was the Serb response? We are so ill informed that I only discovered it in an article from the *New York Times* of 8 April, which somebody sent me in one of the thousands of letters that I have received. In that article Steven Erlanger from Belgrade said: 'Just before the bombing the Serbian parliament rejected NATO troops in Kosovo ... it also supported the idea of a United Nations force to monitor a political settlement there.' The argument is about whether the answer is NATO troops or an international force.

We all speak from experience. I was a Member of the House at the time of the Suez crisis. The only other Member who can say the same, the right hon. Member for Old Bexley and Sidcup [Sir E. Heath], was then the Government Chief Whip. I was advising Hugh Gaitskell, who did not, as Leader of the Opposition, have a television set. He came to my house to watch Eden's broadcast. I sat with Gaitskell at his house in Hampstead for the whole of Sunday 4 November 1956 and helped him, as a young Member would help a party leader, with his broadcast about Suez. He said: 'There is no doubt about it that the large-scale invasion of Egypt was an act of aggression … We should have been acting on behalf of the United Nations with their full authority … It is not a police action; there is no law behind it. We have taken the law into our own hands. What are the consequences? We have violated the Charter of the United Nations. In doing so we have betrayed all that Great Britain has stood for in world affairs.' The sound and other technicians were listening, riveted, to that broadcast. That represented my commitment, which is that force can be used only by the UN.

We are facing a long war; there is no doubt about that. The war has already spread to Macedonia, Montenegro and Albania and, for all I know, it will spread beyond that. I do not know what the Russians will do. I am told that earlier this afternoon Yeltsin said that Russia would not allow Yugoslavia to be defeated. We cannot rely on Yeltsin – he may be seeking a foreign crisis to get him off a hook, but so may President Clinton.

How will the situation end? With ground troops? The hon. Member for Tatton [Mr Bell], who speaks from great media experience of war, is right – bombing will not work. Troops will therefore be sent in, but if we do that, will it be an occupation, a partition or a protectorate? How will the refugees return? The Opposition properly asked those questions. The right hon. and learned Member for Folkestone and Hythe [Mr Howard] exercised his responsibility as a party spokesman to ask questions that simply have not been answered. Who will pay for the villages to be rebuilt? Those questions are simply brushed aside.

Who wants the war? President Clinton wants the war because he runs NATO. The Prime Minister is continually repeating his commitment to the war. We see pictures of him in the cockpit of aircraft, which make clear his intent. NATO wants the war because it will make it credible. Many times I have heard people say, 'NATO must be credible', and I realise that the war is not so much about the refugees as about NATO's credibility. The KLA wants the war because we are arming it. We joined in a civil war, and armed the KLA. I will not say that the arms trade wants a war, but there is big business to be made from replacing the armour that has been used.

As for the media, there are daily press conferences. I personally think that it is an insult to our intelligence to personalise all conflicts as if, somehow, shooting Saddam Hussein and Milosevic would return peace to the Middle East and the Balkans. What folly to engage in such schoolboy politics. There are complex historical conditions. If Milosevic were shot, somebody else would come along who is just the same, because the Serbs are united. The history is ignored.

The Serbs are demonised. There is demonisation of the enemy in war; we must make out that every Serb is a criminal and it is therefore our duty to kill him. The Serbs are people; people know that they may not like their own government. The hon. Member for Tatton said that many Serbs want to get rid of Milosevic, yet they are all demonised.

Critics are denounced as appeasers – I have heard that before. I was accused by Bernard Braine, whom I dearly love, of being 'Nasser's little lackey' during Suez. He apologised so many times afterwards that I felt quite sorry for him. Critics were always accused of being an agent of the Kremlin, a supporter of the IRA, in favour of Adolf Hitler. That is no way in which to conduct a conflict of this kind.

The peace movement is, of course, ignored.

What is the role of Parliament in this war? We are being told by the government's two chief press officers what is being done, and then told that all parties agree. The right hon. and learned Member for North-

East Fife [Mr Campbell] was fair in saying that he shared my view about the role of Parliament.

There is to be no vote tonight. My Whip has told me, on this great historic occasion, 'Your attendance is requested'– with one line under it. Is it not important to the government to indicate their support? When all we can do is vote on the closure motion, I do not think that many will vote with us – they probably will not – but at least others will be given an opportunity to abstain. I am not so sure whether the government do not want a vote because, although they might not yet find many against them, many – even from the Conservative Party – might not want to go into the Lobby.

We are responsible people. Being a Member of Parliament is a great honour, but it carries responsibility: the responsibility for deciding whether one agrees with the government of the day. This is an ill-thought-out policy. It is not legal in character; it is not moral in its implication. I do not make much of the convoy, because war is bloody and indiscriminate – it always has been and always will be. Hon. Members who want to be spectators of their fate ought to consider very seriously whether, even by abstention, and certainly by not voting, they are assenting to a policy which, in my serious judgement, will not succeed, but which will inflict terrible damage on the Balkans, with which we shall have to live for many years to come.

Wednesday 8 November 2000

I asked Caroline today, because one or two people have said to me, 'Don't you think you should have a permanent nurse?', 'Would you rather have a nurse?' And she said, 'No, I'd rather you looked after

me', and that was such a sweet thing to say. I was really touched by that and it gave me a big boost.

The American presidential election is apparently hung. Gore has got a bigger popular vote than Bush, but it all hinges on Florida, where the American media first of all said Gore had won, then Bush had won, then Gore had won. Actually it was all based on exit polls, and the result depends on postal votes; and there's a recount in Florida. So neither of the candidates can say very much. Ralph Nader got about 3 per cent which probably contributed to the defeat of Gore and will make people angry with him. But as he said on television, 'Well, this is the end of the two-party system and corporate finance', and I agree with him.

George W. Bush was confirmed as President-elect of the United States. Caroline Benn died on 22 November.

Friday 6 September 2002

The Iraq story absolutely dominates everything, particularly as Blair said that we have to pay a 'blood price' for our special relationship with America, which is a horrific, tribal, medieval thing to say. Anyway today I did eleven broadcasts – London, Shropshire, Merseyside, Sheffield, West Midlands, York, Leeds, the Asian Network, Bristol, the *World at One* and, in the evening, *Any Questions?*

CHAPTER SIX

Widower

Tony Benn made his last speech to the House of Commons on 22 March 2001. The debate was on the election of the Speaker and proposals to change the system.

After the death of Caroline the previous year, Tony lived alone for the first time in fifty-one years; the last fourteen years of his life were dominated, politically, by successive international crises. It was, as he often mentioned in his speeches, the self-declared 'new American century of full-spectrum dominance'. He became President of the Stop the War movement and gained a new younger following of peace activists; he also at this time acquired an older audience (with more than a sprinkling of political conservatives) through a hectic schedule of theatre appearances around the country, which began as a one-man show and developed into conversations with the writer and presenter Samantha (Sam) Norman. These contributed to the transmogrification of Tony into a national treasure.

From 2001 to 2004 he wrote a weekly comment column for the Morning Star; after 9/11 he also began a punishing round of meetings and rallies arguing against war, first in Afghanistan, then in Iraq. He had personal experience of Iraq dating back to the 1990s during the *dispute between Iraq and Kuwait, when he visited Saddam Hussein and met the Foreign Minister, the Assyrian Christian Tariq Aziz, for whom he subsequently campaigned when Aziz was imprisoned after the Iraq invasion of 2003.*

22 March 2001,
Last speech to the House of Commons

I ask the indulgence of the House. This may be my last speech, so if I am out of order, Mr Speaker, I hope that you will allow me to range widely.

I support the report of the Procedure Committee and the motion proposed by my right hon. Friend the Leader of the House. The report is scholarly and historical; it considers all the arguments. My only difference with it is over the question of a secret ballot. I have always understood that if one votes as oneself, it must be secret. Years ago, when I was canvassing in Bristol, I asked a woman to support me and she replied, 'Mr Benn, the ballet is secret'. I thought of her dancing alone in the bedroom, where no candidate was allowed to know about it. However, when we vote in a representative capacity, people must know what we have done, so I shall vote for the amendment. The Committee has done very well. I hope that the House accepts the report.

The old system had serious difficulties. Although I disagreed strongly with the Father of the House, he carried out his duties with exceptional skill – with panache! I felt that he was the only Member of the House who could have turned the Beefeaters into a fighting force – he showed such passion and commitment to the rules. We got the Speaker we wanted and I hope that, as a result of today's proceedings, we shall get the system we want – the one that I advocated, as the House will recall.

As I have done on previous occasions – when we were electing a Speaker – I want to look a little more broadly at the role of the Speaker. Often, we tend to think of the Speaker in relation only to the Chamber, but the Speaker's role is of much wider importance. Relations between the legislature and the Executive go through the Speaker of the House.

We live in a strange country: we do not elect our head of state; we do not elect the second Chamber. We elect only this House, and even in this House enormous power is vested in the prerogatives. The Prime Minister can go to war without consulting us, sign treaties without consulting us, agree to laws in Brussels without consulting us and appoint bishops, peers and judges without consulting us. The role of the Speaker today compared with that of Mr Speaker Lenthall is that you, Mr Speaker, are protecting us from the triple powers of Buckingham Palace, the Millbank Tower and Central Office, which, in combination, represent as serious a challenge to our role.

Then there is the link between the Commons and the people. I have seen many schoolchildren taken around the House, and have talked to some of them about how it has been a home of democracy for hundreds of years. In 1832, only 2 per cent of the population had the vote. That may seem a long time ago, but it was only eighteen years before my grandfather was born. When I was born, women were not allowed the vote until they were thirty. Democracy – input from the people – is very, very new. The link between popular consent and the decisions of the House can be tenuous.

Furthermore, nowadays, Parliament representing the will of the people has to cope with many extra-parliamentary forces – very threatening extra-parliamentary forces. I refer not to demonstrations, but to the power of the media, the power of the multinationals, the power of Brussels and the power of the World Trade Organisation – all wholly unelected people.

The House will forgive me for quoting myself, but in the course of my life I have developed five little democratic questions. If one meets a powerful person – Adolf Hitler, Joe Stalin or Bill Gates – ask them five questions: 'What power have you got? Where did you get it from? In whose interests do you exercise it? To whom are you accountable? And how can we get rid of you?' If you cannot get rid of the people who govern you, you do not live in a democratic system.

The role of the Speaker has another importance. When the political manifestos are yellowing in the public libraries, a good ruling from the Speaker in a footnote in *Erskine May* might turn out to be one of the guarantees of our liberty.

There are two ways of looking at Parliament. I have always thought that, from the beginning – from the model Parliament – the establishment has seen Parliament as a means of management: if there is a Parliament, people will not cause trouble, whereas, of course, the people see it as a means of representation. Those are two quite different concepts of what Parliament is about. The establishment wants to defuse opposition through Parliament; the people want to infuse Parliament with their hopes and aspirations.

I have put up several plaques – quite illegally, without permission; I screwed them up myself. One was in the broom cupboard to commemorate Emily Wilding Davison, and another celebrated the people who fought for democracy and those who run the House. If one walks around this place, one sees statues of people, not one of whom believed in democracy, votes for women or anything else. We have to be sure that we are a workshop and not a museum.

My next point, if I am not out of order, is that all progress comes, in my judgement, from outside the House. I am in no way an academic, but if I look back over history, I see many advances first advocated outside the House, denounced by people in power and then emerging. Let me use a couple of non-controversial examples. Twenty years ago, Swampy would have been denounced as a bearded weirdy; he will probably be in the next honours list, because the environmental movement has won. Similarly, when that madman, Hamilton, killed the children at Dunblane, the then Conservative Home Secretary banned handguns within six months, because public opinion had shifted. So we are the last place to get the message, and it is important that we should be connected effectively to public will.

There is a lot of talk about apathy, and it is a problem, but it is two sided. Governments can be apathetic about the people, as well as people being apathetic about governments. For me, the test of an effective, democratic Parliament is that we respond to what people feel in a way that makes us true representatives. The real danger to democracy is not that someone will burn Buckingham Palace and run up the red flag, but that people will not vote. If people do not vote, they destroy, by neglect, the legitimacy of the government who have been elected.

May I finish with a couple of personal points? I first sat in the Gallery sixty-four years ago, and my family have been here since 1892 – five of us in four generations, in three centuries – and I love the place. I am grateful to my constituents who have elected me. I am grateful to the Labour Party, of which I am proud to be a member. I am grateful to the socialists, who have helped me to understand the world in which we live and who give me hope. I am also deeply grateful to the staff of the House – the Clerks, the policemen, the security staff, the Doorkeepers, librarians, *Hansard* and catering staff – who have made us welcome here.

May I finish, in order, by saying something about yourself, Mr Speaker? In my opinion, you are the first Speaker who has remained a Back Bencher. You have moved the Speaker's Chair on to the Back Benches. You sit in the Tea Room with us. You are wholly impartial, but your roots are in the movement that sent you here, and you have given me one of the greatest privileges that I have ever had – the right to use the Tea Room and the Library after the election. Unless someone is a Member or a peer, he or she cannot use the Tea Room or the Library, but you have extended the rules by creating the title of 'Freedom of the House', so that the Father of the House and I will be able to use the Tea Room. You will not be shot of us yet. I hope in paying you a warm tribute, Mr Speaker, that you do not think that I am currying favour in the hope that I might be called to speak again because, I fear, that will not be possible.

◄○►

Politically Tony became more and more detached from the UK govern-ments of Tony Blair and Gordon Brown, with their financial conserva-tism and 'Third Way' mantra, which he (correctly) predicted would soon be consigned to oblivion. The Morning Star *offered him a platform:*

The Prime Minister will go down in the history books as the man who created two political parties, and abolished another political party – which is no mean achievement. First he invented 'New Labour', then he renamed the Labour Party which had elected him as its leader as 'Old Labour'. By doing so he seems to think that the Labour Party itself has actually disappeared, although he was re-elected to Parliament in June as the Labour Party candidate.

These manoeuvres have only had one purpose: to distance himself from the trade unions, from socialism and from the record of his predecessors as Labour leaders who became Prime Ministers. Above all he is determined that Britain will never go back to a policy of 'tax and spend', which he believes would alienate Rupert Murdoch and middle England, both of whom he depends upon for support – that strange combination of the *Sun* and those living in the Home Counties who elected Mrs Thatcher three times and who, the spin-doctors believe, will back him now only if he can show himself to be continuing her policies.

All governments tax and spend, and the real question is: who pays the taxes and what are they spent on. If that is not discussed, then the whole argument is meaningless. If pensioners pay through VAT on the necessities when they buy in the shops, and the money raised goes on Trident, that is wrong; but if the wealthy are taxed at a higher rate so as to fund the NHS to provide care for the elderly, that is right.

There is always plenty of money for war and since New Labour came to power it has bombed Iraq, former Yugoslavia and Afghanistan, and paid the bill, but pensioners (many of whom served in the forces in the last world war against Fascism) are still denied an increase in their pensions in line with earnings. The government would (no doubt) respond to this by saying that defence is in the national interest, and you cannot count the cost in time of war. However, we must ask whether those wars were morally right, and what else is also in the national interest which we are currently neglecting.

Most people expect a Labour Government to regard the national interest as including health, education and care of the sick and the old, and to fund these services by taxation based upon ability to pay, rather than leaving them to market forces.

In 1948 the Ministry of Health issued a leaflet to introduce the new National Health Service, which came into existence on 5 July that year. The opening paragraph described it quite clearly under the heading 'What is it? How do you get it?'

It will provide you with all medical, dental and nursing care. Everyone – rich or poor, man, woman and child – can use any part of it. There are no charges except for a few special items. There are no insurance qualifications. But it is not a 'charity'. You are all paying for it, mainly as taxpayers, and it will relieve your money worries in times of illness.

All prescriptions, all dental care, all spectacles, and even wigs, were absolutely free – this at a time when the nation was still suffering the immense damage done during the war; but it showed that the will to act was there, and it was the greatest thing done by that Labour Government.

It was also Labour which made grants available for those who went on to college. The introduction by this government of loans and fees has already discouraged some young people from going into higher education, for fear of landing up with a huge debt hanging like a millstone around their necks in later life.

And Labour it was, when Barbara Castle was in charge of social security, which linked pensions with earnings, funded by a combination of taxation and National Insurance.

Yet now private companies, whose prime responsibility is to their shareholders, are being brought in to run our schools and hospitals. Taxpayers are to be asked to pay for the profits which go to these shareholders, instead of the money going directly back into teachers' or nurses' pay or towards funding new equipment.

In New Labour's last manifesto a pledge was given – as in 1997 – that wealthy people would not be asked to pay more income tax, whereas pensioners are subjected to a means test under the minimum pension guarantee. I hope that the new and long-overdue debate, opened up after the Chancellor's statement last week, about the need for tax increases to fund our public services does indicate a real change of heart by the government, which would win wide public support.

I also hope that ministers can be persuaded to abandon the hideous practice of 'naming and shaming' those public services that do have problems and need to improve their own performance. The way to help them to do this is to listen to those who work in them, see that the necessary funds are available and give some encouragement, instead of attempting to humiliate them in public, which is bound to lower morale and make things worse.

And I am waiting for some public comment by a minister about those private companies which have failed the nation, but which are never, never publicly named or shamed. This government wants to be seen as business-friendly and presumably cannot ever criticise the private sector, in case it undermines public confidence in the privatisation of our public service – a policy which no real Labour Government would ever support.

Saturday 28 June 2003

Drove to Bristol with my editor Ruth and met her twin sister and her nephew Matthew, nineteen, who realised that his best chance of getting into the Festival was to be with me, as my bag carrier. We had a sticker for the car, and with that everyone waved us on through the streets and got to the Festival site at 1.30 and found a place. Everything is done by mobile phone. There are 120,000, 140,000, 160,000 at Glastonbury – an astonishing site, all these little tents, cars, motorbikes, masses of volunteers, all young and the most elaborate, completely informal structure. And lots of stalls. Ruth decided to go away for the day and I was taken to the Left Field, where Bianca Jagger turned up. The Left Field is three times as big as last year and there was a concert going on next door. The noise was unbelievable and I could hardly hear myself talk. I wondered if anybody would come, but there were 2,000 people in the tent. Many questions, including 'What's the point of voting for the Labour Party? It is all hopeless. What are we going to do to get rid of Tony Blair?' And so on. Then to the Green tent, where Mark Thomas, activist and comedian, was chairing a round circle of people. Someone stamped my arm with a tattoo for Save the Children. Someone also gave me a little envelope that said 'War on Want – Screw Poverty' and later, when I opened it, I found a condom inside!

When I got home I was so tired I just dumped my stuff and went straight to bed.

————— ‹○› —————

Tony Benn was a prominent supporter, and sometimes patron, of several charities, including the Guillain-Barré syndrome organisation and Safer Medicines, a charity that opposes drug-testing on animals.

I have no medical experience or knowledge of any kind, but what I have had a little bit of experience of, as a minister for ten years, is dealing with scientific issues that come up, which very often I couldn't understand, but where the case for an inquiry was strong, I always encouraged that, because there is nothing more conservative, if you know what I mean, than the scientific community, if they think they are being challenged by an idea they don't really like. I think Safer Medicines have made an amazing advance because they've brought together the scientific evidence – it isn't as though we were way on the fringes any more, because 250 Members of Parliament have signed an Early Day Motion calling for an independent validation of the arguments put up by them, and I think that is what we should be calling for. You can't anticipate the research, but I feel quite confident, having attended meetings – I chaired a meeting in Oxford in which this issue came up – I am absolutely confident that the case is a strong enough one to merit an inquiry, and if it does take place and if it does prove that these arguments are valid, then it could have a profound impact on medical research, on medical science, on human health, on the cost of drugs and all the rest of it: it's a very, very important development. My experience of progress, if I finish with this, is very simple: if you come up with a new idea, like votes for women for example, you're ignored. If you go on after you've been ignored, you are absolutely stark staring bonkers – I've had a touch of that myself in life. If you go on after that, you're very, very dangerous: they locked up the suffragettes. And then there's a pause, and then you can't find anyone at the top who doesn't claim to have thought of it in the first place. That is how progress is made, and I have a feeling that Safer Medicines are at the pause stage, just before the guys at the top recognise it.

―――――――――◄○►――――――――

In the Morning Star *in 2001 Tony returned to an earlier theme – industrial democracy – via the vogue for 'outsourcing' work.*

One of the most powerful weapons now used by business against labour is the management consultant, brought in, we are always assured, only to recommend ways of improving efficiency and productivity. However, the real purpose of the consultant is often to downsize, outsource work to others and invent reasons to lay off those who are employed by the company that has taken them on. This practice of bringing in consultants has grown steadily over the years and is now spreading to the public sector as well, being used as an excuse to break down and privatise operations that have been controlled by democratically elected local authorities, public agencies and even government departments.

A consultant's report can always be presented as being completely objective, since it comes from those who bring special expertise to the job and, being independent, can be trusted to give advice that is not available inside the organisation. In practice, many firms bring in consultants to provide them with arguments for doing what they want to do anyway, and the consultants know this very well and make sure, before they start, of exactly what is required of them. They will carefully check their recommendations with the management that has engaged them before they submit them to the directors, who will then be able to endorse them to their own workforce, who are expected to go along with what is proposed.

The outsourcing of jobs previously done by staff employed in-house can, on the advice of consultants, be steered towards companies with which the consultant already enjoys a special relationship. Where the consultants are asked to follow up their own recommendations with the company, they have power without real responsibility in the organisation.

The main gain of outsourcing to those who suggest it is, of course, that the threat of putting work out to tender can be used to worsen conditions for existing staff. If work is actually put out, then those employed to do it may have lower wages, poorer working conditions and be less protected from redundancy. This was the case when hospital cleaning contracts went out, often lowering the standard of cleanliness for staff and patients alike.

It is high time that the trade-union movement challenged this whole philosophy and rediscovered the case for industrial democracy, which would give those who actually do the work the chance to get the information they require, discuss and decide for themselves how the work that they do could be more efficient, and what they need – and expect – from their own management.

The British Labour movement has a fine tradition of arguing for greater industrial democracy, as for example in 1910, when Thomas Straker, the secretary of the Northumberland miners, in evidence recommending public ownership of the pits to the Sankey Commission, said:

Any administration of the mines, under nationalisation, must not leave the mine worker in the position of a mere wage-earner, whose sole energies are directed by the will of another … He must have a share in the management of the industry … He must feel that the industry is run by him in order to produce coal for the use of the community, instead of profit for a few people.

The Union of Post Office Workers, now a part of the CWU, had the same commitment. With the far higher level of education, technical knowledge and understanding that there is today, it must be obvious that the knowledge and skills required in-house far exceed those which can be imported by this new breed of management consultant, who seem to hover like vultures above us and tell us what to do, entrapping us all in a nightmare of bureaucracy that is both inefficient and destructive of our own powers of imagination and capacity to innovate.

Nor would this in any way threaten the genuine management expertise that exists in-house, for most workers respect good managers and want to support them. In any case, managers are themselves under threat from the consultants, who may well be undermining their own authority and their jobs, too.

New Labour is collapsing around us in a flurry of gimmicks and mutual recrimination. However, all those of us who are looking beyond the present impasse must necessarily be coming up with positive and practical solutions that can also win widespread support; and we must re-establish faith in the contribution the Labour movement can make to benefit those who use the services that are provided, as well as those who actually provide them.

Privatisation is the life-blood of the consultants. We should turn our back on both and believe in ourselves again.

———◄○►———

The events of 11 September 2001

The huge tragedy of wholly innocent people caught up in the bombing of New York and Washington has quite properly occupied the attention of everyone in Britain. The messages of sympathy that have been sent are real and moving. No one could have ever imagined that they would see pictures showing such devastation in America, which is by far the most powerful nation the world has ever seen.

We are used to watching television news bulletins showing Hanoi being bombed, or Baghdad or Belgrade, but America we all thought was exempt, and now that has changed and the world will never be the same again. For what was destroyed was not just the World Trade Center and the Pentagon, but the illusion that any nation, great or small, could act without consequences. The old ideas about defence have been shattered. Traditionally nations protected themselves from attack by threatening to kill their enemy, but that does not work when you are up against a suicide bomber who is ready to die and take you with him, and however many smart bombs a country may have, they don't help, either. The assumed supremacy that we associate with industrial muscle and atomic warheads may just be an illusion.

Indeed, one of the surest casualties of this tragedy has been the Star Wars project, which would have been no help at all against such an attack. Whereas, if the sixty-billion-dollar cost of it was diverted to reduce world poverty, that might just help to reduce the risk of conflict. Predictably Bush warns of retaliation, but against whom and with what?

Osama Bin Laden is the suspect most often mentioned, but we are not often reminded that he was trained and financed by the CIA when President Bush's father was in charge of it. Bin Laden was sent to Afghanistan, his headquarters built for him by the Americans, to be a 'freedom-fighter' against the Russians, who at the time occupied that country. In Moscow at the time he was seen as a terrorist, which is how he is now seen in Washington.

After the attacks on the US Embassies in Africa three years ago Clinton launched a massive missile attack on a factory in the

Sudan, which everyone now knows had nothing whatever to do with the original assault. For all I know, the suicide bomber may have seen what he did this week as retaliation for that.

There can be no end to revenge killings, and when the White House advises Israelis and Arabs to call for a ceasefire and start peace talks, it is right – and maybe they should take their own advice now. Certainly Israel, which has an immensely powerful army itself, is learning that its forces cannot quell the Palestinian intifada, and America too may have to learn that lesson.

The Prime Minister's grave warnings and pledges of full support for the President suggest that if the United States does strike back with force, British planes may be made available to join them. When Parliament meets today [14 September 2001] I hope that the danger of that is spelled out in the debate. It is right that the House of Commons is being recalled, as was the US Congress, because we need to gather experience and wisdom from all over the world, if we are to respond in the right way to this tragedy. This is why the General Assembly should also meet in an emergency session, in which the real underlying causes of this crisis can be explored.

We owe it to the Americans who have suffered, as well as to ourselves and the rest of the world, to think before we take immediate military action that might just escalate into a world conflict that no one can control.

—◦—

The American/UK/Europe response to 9/11 – to launch a military strike in Afghanistan in October 2001 against the Taliban and al-Qaeda bases there – was initially successful, but was soon to be complicated by a second war in early 2003 against Baghdad, with all the long-term consequences for the region that Tony Benn and others warned against. In July 2002 Tony wrote the following piece.

Parliament has now adjourned until October and with it has gone the possibility of MPs holding the government to account for what it is doing, leaving it free to plan a war against Iraq which may start at any time. The Prime Minister has said that no decision has yet been taken, but every time President Bush speaks, he reaffirms his determination to launch that war and he expects Britain to give its support. The exact date on which the bombing will begin may not have been decided in Washington, but detailed military cooperation between the Pentagon and the Ministry of Defence must be taking place on a daily basis.

It is reported that the first stage will be a massive series of air attacks, to be followed by an invasion involving over 200,000 US troops. Apparently British forces numbering over 20,000 may be added, but it is the political support from London and not the military contribution from this country that the Americans really need.

This war will be in defiance of the UN charter, which only authorises the use of military force when it has been decided by the Security Council, with the support of the five permanent members, including France, Russia and China. If Britain joins in, we will be guilty of conducting an act of aggression and committing war crimes against those innocent civilians who are bound to be killed ... The responsibility for this will lie with the Prime Minister personally, who will have taken this decision without the authority of a vote in the House of Commons.

The new Archbishop of Canterbury, Dr Rowan Williams, appointed this week, has made it absolutely clear that he will not support this war unless the UN has given its authority.

I do not know whether the Prime Minister appreciates the enormity of the choice that he would be making to defy the UN, break international law and kill people at the behest of President Bush. If, in the event, he does take that view, he could well forfeit his claim to the support of all those across the whole spectrum of British opinion who see war as a moral issue. He will also destroy his own moral authority and relieve us of any obligations we may have to respect him. For so long as he can maintain his majority in Parliament he will, in law, be able to retain his office and his power, but from that moment he will have lost his right to be believed or trusted, and the only people who can save him from making such a disastrous mistake are other Labour MPs, whether the House is in recess or not. This is why over these summer months a massive public campaign is required to alert all ministers and MPs to their duty, and to warn them of their own responsibility to those who elected them.

Quite apart from the moral arguments against this war, the consequences in the Middle East and elsewhere, if it takes place, would inflame the whole region. This could well lead to the toppling of some regimes that have been obedient to America, but whose populations deeply resent the impact of American imperialism on their lives.

A war with Iraq, which would certainly alienate Russia and China, and many of our European partners as well, could cost Tony Blair his job, undermine public support for the government as a whole and inflict untold suffering on millions of people. It must be prevented.

◄○►

What joining the euro would mean for Britain, February 2002

The attempt by the European Central Court to censure Chancellor Gordon Brown for his plans to invest public money in the public services, together with the threat, now withdrawn, to impose a fine on Chancellor Schröder for exceeding the approved limit for public expenditure (in part forced by the high level of unemployment in Germany) is a stark reminder of what joining the euro means for Europe, and what it would really mean for us.

After all the hype about the new euro currency and how exciting it is, and how convenient it would be for British holidaymakers on the continent if Britain joins, the real issue has at last surfaced. It is about the total loss of democratic control of our economy which we would experience if we did opt for the new currency.

The Maastricht Treaty, which we have already signed, lays down, under the so-called 'stability pact', the limits of borrowing and spending that are permitted in every country which ratified the treaty. Although we have not signed up to the euro itself, we are still subject to the same rules, which is why we are being forced to undergo an extensive programme of privatisation.

The second problem that will soon have to be confronted by countries in the Eurozone is that they will all be subject to the same interest rates, also set up by the Central Bank. It should be obvious that conditions vary from country to country, and that a set rate may be too high in one country and too low in another, with disastrous results that could not be corrected. The Maastricht Treaty also makes it an offence for any government even to try to influence the decisions of the Central Bank. Thus if German, French, Italian, Spanish or British trade unionists, or even industrialists, were to appeal to their own elected governments to reduce interest rates in order to save jobs, the Finance Ministers of the governments they have elected would be unable to do so. This in turn would undermine all public confidence in the democratic process, because if the parliaments we elect are powerless, then why should anyone bother to vote? If they don't vote, that is the end of democracy itself, and the way is open for some demagogue to take over. Inevitably people here who were suffering would look for a scapegoat. It would be much easier to whip up hostility to the Germans or the French than to understand the real nature of the problem, which would be that the system itself was at fault.

And the dangers would not stop there. The discovery that we were governed by bankers we did not elect, and could not remove, would inevitably lead to the crudest form of nationalism. I can even visualise a breakdown in Europe along the lines of that in former Yugoslavia, with all the subsequent consequences.

I suspect, without any inside knowledge of any kind, that no Chancellor of the Exchequer could possibly want to give up the power he has to control our own economy. Likewise no Governor of the Bank of England would want to see his own role downgraded to that of a mere branch manager, taking all his orders from head office in Frankfurt.

Put very crudely, the euro question is fundamental to whether we still believe in democracy itself, or whether we have abandoned it, entrusting our future to bankers who do not share our objectives and are determined to control us in the interest of capital. For they will use deflation as the simplest way of weakening labour to boost profits for their real constituents – the shareholders of Europe and the world.

The new opium of the people

Every hour the BBC and ITV give us an update on the business news, with movements of the Dow Jones and the Footsie 100, together with information on the fluctuations between the value of the dollar, the euro and the pound. This is always explained to us as if it was the main interest to all of the viewers, presumably to help pensioners rush out to sell their dollars and buy euros while the rate is favourable.

Those who wake really early can watch a full half-hour before 6 a.m. on the BBC when financial correspondents in Wall Street and elsewhere report on individual share prices of the major corporations. They do so with all the gravity of a commentary on a service in a cathedral, which in a sense it is, since all this information is part of an ongoing act of worship for those who see money as their god.

I would be very surprised if those who work in the City of London rely on this to guide them in their own decisions, because they are fully equipped with laptops, mobile phones, fax machines and pagers that keep them posted minute-by-minute. And they are probably far too busy gambling with millions to turn on their television sets.

That is one definition of news, but for those who are interested in politics we have a regular diet of lobby correspondents who stand outside Number 10 to keep us fully informed about the prospects of a Cabinet reshuffle, or update us on the argument between Black Rod and the Prime Minister about exactly where he stood during the Queen Mother's funeral, and which front-bencher is expected to come out of the closet within the next few days.

Then there are regular photo opportunities to show one minister reading a book to some school children, another dressed in a white coat leaning over a patient in a hospital that has been built under the private finance initiative, and a tough briefing from the MoD to explain how the Pentagon in Washington absolutely depended on British bombers to carry through their operation to remove Saddam Hussein.

To help us understand all this, the media have a battery of academic experts on call, who can fill in the background with a few statistics. These are then further explored by a round table of pollsters and political pundits, who can be relied upon to assess the political significance for the party leaders and dismiss a few maverick MPs and agitators who, we are assured, can be safely disregarded as having no influence on their own parties.

When Michael Meacher courageously and correctly indicated this week that he felt that he was a lone voice in the wilderness, arguing that the environment was not taken seriously by the government, he was shining a welcome shaft of light on the world of spin, helping us to see through it all. Predictably, however, his comments were immediately brushed aside by an unidentified spokesman from Number 10 whose job it is to see that no real debate on the issue was to be allowed.

The environment is a subject that is really too hot to handle, because it poses a threat to those multinationals that make some of their profit by despoiling the planet. Dedicated green campaigners can then be reclassified as eco-terrorists and dealt with under the new legislation passed to deal with the threat posed by Osama Bin Laden on 11 September.

The real opium of the people today is no longer religion, but the extensive coverage of sport, the silly game-shows, confession and synthetic confrontation programmes which encourage people to tell all, and *Big Brother*, which encourages us to hope that we shall see all. These are interspersed with films spattered with violence and sex that must explain the behaviour of those for whom killing apparently seems quite normal.

The Director General of the BBC, who has been pushing through the digital revolution, has reassured us that BBC4 is for those who want to think. This leaves people like me, who still only have BBC1 and BBC2, with apparently no legitimate reason to believe that they will be encouraged to think by either of those mainstream outlets.

Meanwhile life goes on outside this closed circle, and no one knows it better than the trade-union movement, whose interests and activities are systematically ignored unless there is some form of industrial action, in which case the BBC will revert to its old language and talk about the 'barons' and the 'bosses' of the trade unions holding the country to ransom.

But let us note and remember the anti-war movement, which was dismissed a few months ago as a typical minority of troublemakers and now commands the support of the new Archbishop of Canterbury and a majority of the citizens of this country.

------------◄○►------------

Friday 3 October 2003

The meter man arrived early this morning. He said the job he had enjoyed doing best of all was working in the sewers. He said sewers

were unbelievable – you could drive a car through them. He said that all the excrement turns into black silt; you waded through black silt. I've always thought sewers were quite romantic. It would make a marvellous programme.

Rory Bremner rang – he and his researcher want to come and have a talk about a Channel 4 special coming up ... I'd given a little thought to it, and I did say to him that I thought the friendly, smiling Blair wasn't quite right, because there was a tough authoritarian nature to him, which ought to be reflected. He agreed with that.

The Iraq survey group set up by the Americans, which has cost God knows how many millions of dollars, has found absolutely no weapons of mass destruction, so not only is Blair in trouble in Britain, despite his huge conference success at Bournemouth, but Bush is in trouble in America – and not only from the Democrats. So it may be that this war will bring down Bush. I doubt it'll bring down Blair because there is no provision for it. Those who opposed the war – not that one wants to say 'I told you so' – certainly do stand tall.

◄○►

The royal prerogatives, July 2002

The system whereby the Prime Minister appoints the bishops and archbishops, in the name of the Queen, makes the Church of England the only church in the Anglican communion worldwide which is nationalised, since the Church of Wales was disestablished in the 1920s and the Scottish Episcopalian Church makes its own appointments. From King Henry VIII's point of view, taking over the Church in 1533 was a brilliant move because it allowed him to put a priest in every pulpit, in every parish, every Sunday, telling the faithful that God wanted them to do what the King wanted them to do, and the Church was then the mass media and was kept under tight control.

The King appointed the bishops and the archbishops, and even today every bishop on appointment has to swear homage to the Crown, using the following words: 'I do hereby declare that your Majesty is the only supreme governor of this your realm, in spiritual and ecclesiastical things as well as in temporal', so that to become a bishop you have to deny the legitimacy of democracy and are rewarded with a seat in the House of Lords.

Nowadays all royal prerogatives are exercised by the Prime Minister and, when there is a vacancy, a committee representing the Church puts forward two names and the Prime Minister chooses the one he or she wants – or can even ask for further names – despite the fact that, by law, the PM is not required to be a member of the Church of England, or even a Christian, and could indeed be a Catholic, Methodist, Jew, Muslim or atheist.

If any Prime Minister were to announce today that he intended to nationalise the Roman Catholic Church, the Methodists, Baptists or Congregationalists, take over the synagogues or mosques and appoint the rabbis and imams, the idea would be universally denounced because it would completely destroy the independence of those religions and their ability to criticise the government on moral grounds, which is exactly the problem facing the established Church of England.

That the Synod recently voted to keep this system unchanged tells us a lot about how undemocratic Britain is, which is why the Prime Minister must be delighted, because he appoints the ministers in his government, members of the House of Lords and the Chairman of the Labour Party (who used to be elected). He knows that any ambitious young priest who might hope one day to become a bishop will never dare to criticise his government. The Queen also likes it because, to make up for the fact that she is not elected, the Archbishop of Canterbury, at her coronation, speaks of her as God's choice for the throne.

It also means that when there is a war in which British troops are involved, Anglican chaplains will bless the soldiers as they go to battle, and by describing it as a 'just war' use God's name to legitimise the killing of those innocent civilians who become victims of the bombing of their towns and villages.

The Church likes it because the bishops sit in the House of Lords and, without being elected, decide upon the laws we are expected to follow. They enjoy a privileged position in our society, and it can be argued that these privileges make this a Christian country, without the need to preach and convert people to accept the message of Jesus and make it relevant to their lives.

The role of religious leaders as teachers, alerting us to the moral factors in decision-making, preaching brotherhood, internationalism and peace, is very important, and indeed the socialist faith owes much to Christian teaching because it has encouraged people to believe that, if we are all equal in the eyes of God, we ought to enjoy that equality in our political and economic lives as well.

Many devout people have been ready to die for their faith, just as socialists have been, but historically we know that, on other occasions, religious leaders tell people to kill for their doctrine, and that is a threat to the survival of the human race.

So when the Synod voted to keep the Church as part of the state machine, they abandoned their responsibilities as religious teachers and chose to kneel before the Queen, the government and those who own the wealth that buys them the privileges which the bishops want to share in the House of Lords.

The Bible tells many stories about kings who had power, and prophets who preached righteousness and often challenged the kings in what they did. In modern Britain, however, the kings appoint the prophets and in this way obliterate the prophetic message that we desperately need, if the human race is to survive in this dangerous world. It is worth noting that many good Christians reject the whole idea that the state should control their Church.

Indeed, if we are ever to get peace in the world, all religious leaders should aim to free themselves from nationalism and jointly excavate the foundations of all faiths, which are rooted in a commitment to preserve life on this earth, by encouraging good and discouraging evil – a message that has particular relevance today.

————————◇————————

Saturday 9 April 2005

The more I think about the Rover collapse, the more I think it's an absolute scandal. The Phoenix consortium bought Rover for £10, assuming all the debts. The directors absolutely ladled out money to themselves and allowed the company to go bust; probably hoped that the government would bail them out anyway. So in Longbridge, one of the great motor manufacturing plants in the world until forty years ago, there are just unfinished vehicles. It confirms everything that I have come to believe; that the government has no industrial policy whatever, and Blair and Brown going there is just a gimmick.

Partly out of curiosity, having watched the Pope's funeral, and trying to understand the country I live in, I watched the wedding of Charles and Camilla. It was a civil wedding in the Guildhall in

Windsor. You saw the guests arriving, a few rather straggly people outside who'd been issued with Union Jacks, waving them in a desultory way. I'm not saying anyone wishes ill to the couple, but I wouldn't have said there was any sense of excitement, not in any way comparable to the attitude of the Polish delegation in Rome yesterday to the death of the Pope.

Then a Rolls-Royce arrived and went back to St George's Chapel for the blessing. I really do feel we've been taken back to Edwardian Britain. Under Blair we've gone back eighty, ninety years, all these toffs in their fancy clothes. No one's embarrassed about wealth any more, and the general public just stand there, with the police watching them, with flags, just waving. They're treated like idiots and imbeciles and servants and slaves.

◄○►

Friday 17 September 2004

Dinner in London with Jonathan Dimbleby, Liz Forgan and David Starkey and some of the BBC people. Then went on to do *Any Questions?* at Westminster School. We had a question, obviously, on hunting, where on the whole the audience was against it. Then there was Iraq and there was tumultuous applause against the war; then education (I was asked about Westminster School); and about whether Blair should resign. I managed to get in my joke about Batman and Bush. I said, 'Oh yes, the security situation is very serious, Batman got into Buckingham Palace, and in America Bush got into the White House! We're in deep trouble!' Then I introduced Lord Button, a composite character of Lord Butler and Lord Hutton, and said, 'Whenever anything goes wrong, Lord

Button is called out of retirement and proves the government is not responsible.'

Thursday 12 October 2006

Headlines on the news bulletins: General Sir Richard Dannatt, who is the Chief of the General Staff, has given an interview to the *Daily Mail* saying, in effect, that the war was poorly planned, that it was totally idealistic to think you could set up a liberal democracy in Iraq, and that the presence of British troops there was exacerbating the situation rather than helping, and we should get out soon ... It has transformed the whole situation, because Blair dare not sack him and what he's said no doubt reflects the view of the army and a lot of other people.

————◦————

CHAPTER SEVEN

Grandfather

*Tony Benn was blessed with nine grandchildren – who christened him
'Dan Dan' – and it was conversations with them that inspired him to
address the issues facing the twenty-first-century generation through
their eyes. He found youngsters genuinely inspiring and motivating.
Some of the school pupils and students he had employed in his office in
the 1980s and 1990s (the Teabags: certificated members of The Eminent
Association of Benn Archive Graduates) came from far and wide to
attend his funeral in March 2014. Artists and musicians – and in one
case a young inventor – sought him out to paint his portrait, set his
speeches to music or ask his advice about their love lives, while he held
court in the flat to which he moved for the last few years of his life.*

*His diary ceased in 2009, due to illness, but the last entries illustrated
his lifelong curiosity and interest in everyday things and people – the
'university of life' – which he preferred to the formal education of his youth.*

I have never indulged in any drugs – other than my pipe; my generation
and the one that followed did not experience the easy availability of
drugs on the streets of Britain. The idea that people find excitement
through drugs worries my Puritan conscience.

I recognise that drugs are widely used, but policies designed to criminalise them and abolish them by force of law, as well as eradicate their production, have failed either to reduce their use in this country or reduce the production of opium in, for example, Afghanistan.

Prohibition in America in the 1920s, designed to make alcohol illegal and to imprison and punish those who bought and sold it, is perhaps the most vivid example of a policy that proved to be a total failure and had to be abandoned.

One of the reasons was that during Prohibition trade in alcohol was taken over by criminals and created a gangster world that did more damage than the alcohol itself.

A dear friend of mine, who was a High Court judge, told me that attempts to criminalise drugs have failed, and were bound to fail. He pointed out that criminalisation has created the same underworld, with all its associated dangers.

And talking recently to a former prison governor, I found him saying a similar thing. People are convicted for drugs offences and then sent to prison, where drugs are readily available.

I once asked a senior director of a major tobacco company what would happen if cannabis were legalised. He told me that plans had been prepared to enable them to trade in cannabis, as they did in cigarettes.

Of course some drugs are more dangerous than others, but I have finally become persuaded that the case for decriminalisation is overwhelming. One of the reasons that MPs – with some notable and brave exceptions – are so nervous about coming out in favour of it is that they would be subjected to media vilification.

The drugs trade is now a huge international industry – and some economies seem almost to depend on it – run by groups who have acquired political power out of the wealth that they have accumulated.

One thing is clear: if drugs were decriminalised, the trade would become more traditional in nature, and the tax that could be imposed at the retail end could provide revenue to be used for social purposes (as tobacco revenue is today).

I put this in a cautious way because I have not felt able to campaign openly and consistently for a policy that I think has become inevitable. It will yield benefits to society that hitherto we have denied on the grounds that enforcement of laws should be allowed to work.

My generation accepts that indulgence in tobacco and abuse of alcohol are a threat to public health – no one can deny it – but no government has yet felt able to ban them completely as criminal activities, because to do so would provoke a huge outcry, would create thousands of prisoners and require a huge policing operation. For these reasons I have come to the conclusion that decriminalisation of 'recreational' drugs, which my grandchildren's generation find no more objectionable than alcohol or tobacco, should be introduced, combined with relevant public health warnings.

In reaching a final verdict, I am very much guided by my grandchildren's views – I trust their judgement more easily than my own – on a subject which politicians, who will have to make the decision, are so reluctant to discuss honestly and openly.

◀◦▶

Tuesday 9 June 2009

My car was impounded this morning. I had to go to the Chelsea car pound to collect it. It cost £260.

The guy who took all the particulars was reading the Bible, so I commented upon that; and he was a Nigerian Pentecostal. He said

the Bible is absolutely true, and gay activities are condemned in the Bible, and the Bible is the Spirit. I said, 'Who created God?' and he said God was a spirit that had always been there, and God didn't create the world in seven days, he created it in six days and on the seventh day he rested ... A little theology in the middle of a horrible experience of having your car impounded made it more tolerable.

◄◦►

The IT Generation

All of my grandchildren, like everyone of their generation, take the Internet and its social possibilities for granted. The technicalities of using it are hard for parents and grandparents to master, but it has helped to create the best-informed generation in history and gives them freedom to exchange information and compare interests across the world.

This very fact has made it a deadly threat to the powerful. Throughout history control of communication and information has been crucial to political control. Dictators use that power over information to dominate their people, even if there is no provision for democracy.

The Church in the early days maintained its power because it was run by clerks who were literate; the Heresy Act of 1401 made it a criminal offence for a lay person to read the Bible. If anybody had an opportunity to study it, they could challenge the authority of the Pope.

Bishop Tyndale, the dissident Christian, lost his life, and Mercator, the revolutionary map-maker, was imprisoned because they gave ordinary people the opportunity to challenge the information propagated by the powerful.

The power of the priesthood eventually came up against the secular power of the King and so Henry VIII nationalised the Church; the Anglican Church then exercised its new power by telling the faithful that God wanted the King to be King and, as church attendance was compulsory, this was a powerful instrument of control.

The Royal Mail was established in 1660 by Charles II, motivated in part, it is believed, by his desire to open his subjects' letters to find out if they were doing anything that might threaten his authority.

Luke Hansard, who gave his name to the reporting of Parliament, was initially imprisoned for publishing its proceedings. Some courageous advocates for civil liberties and the freedom of the press have campaigned against restrictions – such as the Official Secrets Act – which prevent the public from knowing what governments are doing, while governments want to know what everyone else is doing.

With the growth of radio, the Conservative government of the day made broadcasting a public industry for the same reason that Henry VIII had taken over the Church.

The United States recognised the potential and importance of controlling information globally. When Bill Clinton was in the White House, the Pentagon issued a document called 'Full Spectrum Dominance', which stated that the US intended to establish control in space, land, sea, air and information, of which information was the most important.

The Internet has potentially transformed all that, and my grandchildren's generation is already experiencing the results. Newspapers are losing circulation to the electronic media; half of all Britons read a daily paper now, compared to three-quarters thirty years ago. It is possible to organise international events – such as the Stop the War demonstrations and the G20 protests – on the same day in fifty or sixty countries. And information and opinion can be disseminated instantaneously without the intermediate role of an editor or censor. This is already seen as a threat to established power, which is why China insisted that Google monitor the information it provided in China, and why an electronic intifada is being fought by the Palestinians in their struggle for justice; and why, it has been alleged, the CIA plants damaging information on Wikipedia about people whom they do not like.

I believe that the Internet offers us the best hope ever of getting through to each other and challenging abuses of power, and I am absolutely confident that this generation will use technology – blogging, Facebook, YouTube and Twitter, together with mobile phones and digital cameras – more effectively than has ever been possible before in the eternal struggle for peace and justice.

The global village can be experienced on every London bus. People from all corners of the earth are momentarily brought together in one small community. Globalisation is a fact of life. There is no reversing the change that it has brought about. But I prefer the word 'internationalism' to describe what is happening rather than 'globalisation', which has tended to be used to justify the reach of the international corporations worldwide. For in the global village there are many religions, races and common problems that now receive attention.

A hundred years ago news of a famine in some far-off corner of the globe would probably have never reached you; if it did, it would be the result of a despatch sent by sea, of interest only to the Foreign Office. I remember when I was a little boy on holiday at Stansgate, Essex, my father was on the telephone, shouting. I asked my mother and she said, 'Father is talking to the Viceroy of India, in Delhi.' So I wasn't surprised that he had to shout. It was only later that I realised that he, as Secretary of State for India, was responsible to Parliament for the government of India, including what is now Pakistan, Bangladesh and Burma. We once had a visitor from India – the Maharajah of Alwar – who gave me a turban and prince's outfit. He was later murdered.

Today a famine in Somalia or Ethiopia is a famine in your village. You hear about it at once, on television, through the Net and on the phone. Over half the global population now uses mobile phones, and it is impossible to escape responsibility for helping to deal with famine, even if only because it and associated instability are a threat to the security of everyone. Globalisation has changed the world for ever. My generation must come to terms with it or be outdated and irrelevant.

But global power is not new at all, for the history of empires from the beginning of time has been about rule across the world by the strongest nations over the weakest in order to acquire resources, cheap labour and markets. This applied to the Greek and Roman Empires, to Tamerlane's conquests stretching from Central Asia to the Mediterranean, to the Ottoman, the British and now the American Empire; and the arguments in favour of imperialism were identical to those put forward in support of globalisation.

Indeed, when the war in Iraq is recognised – even by the then chief American banker Alan Greenspan – as having been about oil, the question arises: why not buy the oil from Iraq, instead of invading it in order to get control by force?

The answer is that globalisation today manifests itself, as did the old empires of the past, in military-industrial might, which is quite prepared to resort to violence if it thinks it necessary for the preservation of its interests.

China has already become a superpower, India is close on its heels, Brazil is big enough to qualify. This will fundamentally alter the balance of power in the world. In my lifetime I have seen the British

Empire disappear and its replacement, the American Empire, begin its relative decline. American supremacy may soon be replaced by Chinese or Indian.

Neo-liberal globalisation is often presented, quite falsely, as the means by which the rich and powerful can help the poor; any suggestion that it is immoral or self-interested is rejected as crude propaganda. But the price is paid by the exploited workers, and often the environment, through degradation of the land. It benefits a very limited range of people, for there is no suggestion that the free movement of capital carries with it a requirement for the free movement of people. That would lead to social disruption and would be completely unacceptable politically.

Thus a company – feeling under threat and stretched by international competition – can close its factories in Britain and transfer them to India or Thailand or Malaysia, where overheads and wages are much lower, conferring a benefit on the shareholders and the directors.

But if workers in India, Thailand or Malaysia seek entry to Britain, where the wages are higher, they will be stopped by the immigration authorities and sent straight home, denying them the right to maximise their income.

Internationalism has always been at the core of Labour Party thinking, and socialists have seen their responsibilities to working people in all countries – very often against the interests of their employers in the home country.

In the First World War opposition came from German socialists as well as British socialists and, although overwhelmed by the bellicose propaganda, their solidarity was paralleled by the alliances that united people against the rise of the Nazis in the 1930s.

Similarly, the anti-colonial struggles waged by Indians against the British Empire and by Africans against the European colonialists and apartheid were supported wholeheartedly by the Labour and trade-union movement in Britain.

In the 1950s the Movement for Colonial Freedom (now called Liberation) was the great campaigning organisation, much as the Stop the War movement is now. I was active in MCF, which supported the African National Congress against the apartheid regime in South Africa, and there were French, Belgian and other European socialists who gave similar support to their liberation campaigns, for example during the Algerian War.

I think therefore that globalisation needs to be redefined as modern internationalism, and modern internationalism forces us to see the world as a little spaceship in which all the occupants have a common interest in survival – and that survival requires cooperation.

Cooperation is not only morally right and necessary, but an attempt to prevent it is neither possible long-term, nor acceptable even to the powerful, because they know that they cannot control the poor indefinitely. If they try, bloodshed will inevitably follow.

Communication has been transformed in a generation, whether by air or by airwave. The world is closer to our living rooms than Edinburgh or Penzance or Belfast were when I was born in 1925. Internationalism in practice does more to weld these disparate communities together at home than you perhaps may realise. Muslims who have been isolated as a result of propaganda in Britain now find themselves befriended, supported and encouraged by white socialists and West Indian socialists who live here alongside them, and this is the building, at home, of the foundations of what will be needed all over the world.

It is a lesson that my grandchildren's generation does not need to be taught because they understand it already, particularly in areas where the school population is racially mixed. This may be one issue in which the first truly mixed-race generation have a great deal to teach their parents and grandparents, who may not have come to terms with what has happened, don't understand it and are frightened by it. They are lucky.

————◇————

In a final attack on the EU, Tony reappraised the European Union, which had begun with France, Germany, Italy, Belgium, Netherlands and Luxembourg and had expanded in his lifetime to include almost thirty countries. He called his essay 'the new Roman Empire'.

From the time when Julius Caesar landed in 55 BC and brought us into a single currency with the penny, up to the signing of the Treaty of Rome, Britain's relations with Europe have been central to the political debate in this country and still divide both parties in a way that has threatened their unity.

The immediate issue is the euro and whether Britain should join the European single currency; a secondary, but more important, question is whether we should accept a new European constitution drawn up under the chairmanship of the veteran French politician Giscard d'Estaing. The constitutional implications of European enlargement – which has brought in many Eastern European countries and produced a union of twenty-five, four times the size of the original six – are huge. A third question relates to whether or not Europe should have a common defence and foreign policy, in order, it is argued, that Europe is more united and can act as a counterweight to the United States.

At the outset of the Common Market I opposed it as a rich men's club; subsequently, as a minister, I concluded that it was probably the only way of providing political supervision and control of multinational companies that were bigger than nation states; and I have now moved to the position where I see the EU's present form as representing a threat to democracy in Britain and throughout all the member states of the Union.

Harold Wilson changed his view on the matter, having first been against and then coming out in favour; and so did Mrs Thatcher, who was passionately in favour of Britain's membership in 1975 and signed the treaty that introduced the single market, but later, when out of office, opposed the Maastricht Treaty, the euro and all forms of European integration.

By contrast, Roy Jenkins, Michael Heseltine and Jo Grimond were united in support, as was Ted Heath, who signed the Treaty of Accession in 1972 without the authority of a referendum.

Talking to Ted Heath about this over the years, I have always found his arguments both simple and plainly political, for I have heard him say, 'Europe has had two major wars, costing millions of lives, and now we have got to get together.' And his fierce opposition to the Afghan, Iraq and Yugoslav wars confirmed my view that his position on Europe was based partly on his resentment of America dominating our continent.

That is an argument that has to be taken seriously, but since it raises constitutional questions, it would be intolerable if any steps taken to achieve it were slipped through Parliament without referenda to confirm them. Because these are all huge constitutional matters that involve taking away powers from the electors and transferring them into the hands of those who have been appointed.

Over the centuries Europe has seen many empires come and go: Greek, Roman, Ottoman, French and German, not to mention Spanish, Portuguese and British. Many of the conflicts between European states have arisen from colonial rivalry between imperial powers.

The concert of Europe after the fall of Napoleon, in which countries would negotiate alternatives to war, gave way after 1919 to the League of Nations, dominated by the old imperial powers, and broke down in part because Mussolini's Italy launched a colonial war against Abyssinia in breach of the charter of the League.

After the Second World War, Western establishments had to consider how best to cooperate in rebuilding the continent and, as the Cold War began almost immediately, one of their objectives through NATO was to provide armed forces to prevent the Soviet Union from launching a military attack. It could therefore be argued that the EEC was set up to rebuild Europe on safe capitalist lines, and that NATO was set up to arm the EEC against the military threat that we were told was materialising.

Indeed, a few years ago I heard the former American Ambassador in London speaking at a reception in Speaker's House about the Marshall Plan, which, he openly declared, was an investment to prevent the spread of communism.

As Minister of Technology in 1969, facing the massive multinational corporations and wondering how a nation state could cope with them, I did begin to wonder whether the existence of the EEC might offer some opportunity for political control and ought to be considered for that reason. Such a huge step required popular consent, and that was why in 1970 when we were in opposition and I was free to speak, I argued the case for a referendum to seek the consent of the British people. I discovered that the idea of a referendum was absolutely unacceptable to the Establishment, which was totally opposed to giving the people a direct say in any decisions, least of all one that might frustrate their dream of a Europe controlled by the political elite.

The referendum itself, held in 1975 after Heath had lost the 1974 election, was fought in a way that revealed the imbalance of money and influence on the two sides – the pro-Europe campaign having the support of the Establishment and every single newspaper except the *Morning Star*, and able to command enormous resources; while the anti campaign had to find the cash to hold press conferences and meetings.

Wilson moved me from Industry to Energy immediately afterwards and I found myself on the Council of Energy Ministers, where I served until 1970 and had the opportunity of seeing how the Common Market mechanism worked.

During the British presidency in 1977 I was the President of the Council of Energy Ministers. It is the only committee I have ever sat on in my life where, as a member, or even as President, I was not allowed to submit a document – a right confined to the unelected Commission, leaving ministers like some collective monarch in a constitutional monarchy, able only to say Yes or No.

The Council of Ministers is of course the real parliament, for the directives and decisions take effect in member states without endorsement by the national parliaments. Because it is in effect a parliament, I proposed during my presidency that it should meet in public, so that everyone could see how decisions are reached and what arguments are used. This sent a chill of horror through the other ministers, who feared that it would bring to light the little deals that were used to settle differences, and I lost.

I also came to realise that the EEC – far from being an instrument for the political control of multinationals – was actually welcomed by the multinationals, which saw it as a way of overcoming the policies of national governments to which they objected.

For example, I was advised by the Energy Commissioner that North Sea oil really belonged to Europe, and was told by my own officials that the 1946 Atomic Energy Act in Britain, which gave the then government control of all atomic operations, had been superseded by

Euratom (the European Atomic Energy Community) and that we no longer had any power of control.

I was warned that national support for industrial companies was a breach of the principle of free trade and was threatened with action if I disregarded their rules.

It became clear over the succeeding thirty years that the European Union, as it became, is a carefully constructed mechanism for eliminating all democratic influences hitherto exercised by the electors in the member states; it presents this as a triumph of internationalism, when it is a reversal of democratic gains made in the previous hundred years.

Now, with the Maastricht Treaty, the single market and the stability pact, the Frankfurt bankers (who are also unelected) can take any government to court for disregarding the Maastricht Treaty, while the Commission is now engaged in pursuing cases against the elected German and French governments for breaking the strict limits on public expenditure under the stability pact.

If the new European constitution comes into effect, other powers will pass from the parliaments we elect to the Council, Commission and Central Bank, and people here and everywhere in Europe will come to realise that whoever they vote for in national elections cannot change the laws that they are required to obey.

This is the most deadly threat to democracy and, if qualified majority voting removes the current veto system, any government could be outvoted and overruled and the people it was elected to represent would have no real say. Moreover, if the development of an independent foreign and defence policy takes place, we could be taken to war by decisions made elsewhere than in our own parliaments.

Not only is this a direct denial of democratic rights, but it removes the power of governments to discourage revolution or riot, on the grounds that a democratic solution is possible. Then the legitimacy and the stability of any political system come into question.

I am strongly in favour of European cooperation, having presented a bill for a Commonwealth of Europe that would include every country in our continent, as the basis for harmonisation by consent of the various parliaments, just as the UN General Assembly reaches agreements that it recommends should be followed.

The case for a European constitution and currency is also presented as a move beyond nationalism, which has brought such anguish to Europe. But I fear that it will stimulate nationalism, when angry people discover that they are forced to do things they do not want to and are tempted to blame other nations, when the fault actually lies with the system itself.

Federations come and go, as we have seen in the Soviet Union and Yugoslavia, and I do not rule out the opportunity that the European Federation may break up amidst hostility between nations, which is the exact opposite of what we are told will happen.

The idealism of the old

Young people are often considered as either idealistic or cynical and apathetic, while the old are often pessimistic. To my surprise and delight I am rediscovering idealism as I enter my eighty-fifth year.

Pessimism is understandable when brutality is all around, forever tempting you to believe that all is lost, that the hopes of youth for a better world have been dashed by experience and that those who still cherish those hopes are out of touch with reality. The human race, it is easy to believe, is just a collection of animals fighting for survival, power and wealth, and it will never adopt the policies necessary to build a better world.

It is easy for the old to use their experience to justify their pessimism by saying to the young, 'If you knew what we know, you would stop all this foolish talk about building a better world and come to recognise that we live in a jungle where you will have to fight for your own interests.'

But this argument cannot be used against old people who retain their idealism despite the experience they have had and, indeed, find that their own experience justifies hope and encourages dreams rather than destroys them. Jack Jones, the trade-union leader who died in April 2009, and Helen John, the anti-nuclear activist, come to mind.

All real progress throughout history has been made by those who did find it possible to lift themselves above the hardship of the present and see beyond it to an ideal world – some Utopia that gave them hope and the strength to carry on.

This hope has been proved real by every struggling group: the trade unionists who were sent as convicts to Australia for swearing an oath to an 'illegal' union; the suffragettes, imprisoned for their campaign to get women the vote; the many leaders and movements which fought for freedom from their colonial masters; those who fought and defeated apartheid in South Africa; and now the environmentalists who are taking on the global establishment.

This is not to argue for the sort of Panglossian optimism that suggests that you should not worry because everything will end up for the best, because that is the very opposite of the truth.

But pessimism is a prison into which you incarcerate yourselves, removing any desire to join in meeting the challenges which face the human race, and thereby handing over all the power to those who now exercise it at your expense – and who have been corrupted by that power.

Every student of history learns about the corruption of power, but don't forget that there is also the corruption of powerlessness, by which I mean that those who think they have no power, from weakness, hand over the real power they do have to the powerful and thus become complicit in their own oppression.

Looking back on my life, I have come to appreciate the crucial importance of encouragement, remembering the teachers who encouraged me, and the experienced MPs who did the same when I arrived as a youngster in Parliament. When you are encouraged you can do so much better, and when you are put down you know the motive – to keep you under control.

That is why the powerful encourage cynicism, because cynicism helps to keep people away from progressive movements. By contrast, those who believe in themselves, and in the justice of their cause, can only mobilise the movements to which they belong by tapping the fuel of hope which carries those movements forward. Hope is essential even if it is often dashed.

From the beginning of time in the hearts of everyone in every civilisation there have always been two flames burning, the flame of anger against injustice and the flame of hope that we can build a better world.

The best thing the old can do is fan both flames.

I am happy to confess that the visions I had as a youth for peace, justice and democracy worldwide have become more important to me, now that I have had eighty-plus years of experience and I cannot be dismissed on the grounds that when I grow up I will see things differently.

If that is the only argument that I have to face, then I am quite content to admit that I have still not decided what to do when I grow up. Even if I live to a hundred I would still be growing up – right to the moment that my body goes up in flames in the crematorium. And my grandchildren can then decide whether I was right or wrong.

———————◦———————

In Letters to my Grandchildren, *Tony, increasingly aware of his mortality, wrote:*

> I am beginning to think more and more about coming to terms with death. And young people must hope that they get old one day, to avoid dying young!
>
> Getting used to the idea that death is natural inevitably leads to the conclusion that it is also necessary, because the thought of living for ever would be a life sentence (if you know what I mean).
>
> In contrast to the Victorians, our society talks about sex a lot but about death very little and, because of this, death is more mysterious and frightening than it ought to be.
>
> I have become convinced that the right to die is a human right. Although there are problems about legalising it with no conditions attached, I assume and hope that my doctor will help me out when my quality of life has disappeared and I am a burden to myself and to you all.
>
> In talking of old age I mean the period between a fit and active life and the moment of death.
>
> Nature requires the fit and active to procreate, and the desires for sex and love are implanted in our minds to make that possible. (It has sometimes been said that men offer love in return for sex, and women offer sex in return for

love, but it is a cynical way of looking at how real relationships are created and survive.)

When I got married my dad said, 'Don't forget to keep a huge balance of affection in the bank because you will need it', and how very wise he was because, as you will all find out, relationships involve stress and strain and temptation, and the possibility that these might lead to a break.

The concept of old age since even my parents' generation has changed dramatically. The sixty-year-old pensioner is the new middle-aged. The extraordinary improvement in living conditions and medical care, and the increased longevity that has brought, makes it even more absurd now to think of retirement at sixty or sixty-five as a process of winding down until the curtain falls shortly after. And that poses all sorts of social and ethical challenges which your parents, and you, will face.

The young and active will have to finance the hospital treatment, operations and drugs of a large stratum of older people. I have never forgotten Barbara Castle in the Cabinet waving her finger at us all and saying, 'The standard of living we enjoy was earned by those who have now retired and we have a moral responsibility to see that the rising standards we enjoy are shared with those people.' Out of that belief came the policy of pensions linked to earnings, which was abandoned by the Thatcher government and never restored by New Labour.

What do the young get out of taking responsibility for the old? The answer is simple, for it is the sense of identity between the generations and the security that that sense of identity provides. I find it very comforting. But if older people are to be interesting to the young, they have to be *interested* in the young and treat them with respect. I was talking at a meeting recently, when a youngster got up and asked, 'What did you learn from *your* grandparents?' It was a good point! I certainly would not have had the courage to write this letter if I had not benefited so much from what my parents and grandparents taught me. Apart from giving me their love and encouragement, I noticed that they listened to me and treated me with respect, as I hope I do you.

Living as I do 'in a blaze of autumn sunshine' I realise I have learned more from my children and grandchildren than I did from my parents, and therefore look with love and thankfulness on the human family. It seems appropriate to end these letters in a spirit of love and gratitude and sign myself off,

With lots and lots of love,
Dan Dan

Sources and Acknowledgements

The Regeneration of Britain by Anthony Wedgwood Benn
   (Gollancz, 1965)

Speeches by Tony Benn (Spokesman Books, 1974)

Arguments for Socialism by Tony Benn, edited by Chris Mullin
   (Jonathan Cape, 1979)

Arguments for Democracy by Tony Benn, edited by Chris Mullin
   (Jonathan Cape, 1981)

Parliament, People and Power: Agenda for a Free Society by Tony Benn
   (Verso, 1982)

Fighting Back: Speaking Out for Socialism in the Eighties by Tony Benn
   (Hutchinson, 1988)

Common Sense: A New Constitution for Britain by Tony Benn and
   Andrew Hood (Hutchinson, 1993)

Free Radical: New Century Essays by Tony Benn (Continuum, 2003)

Dare to be a Daniel: Then and Now by Tony Benn (Hutchinson, 2004)

Letters to my Grandchildren by Tony Benn (Hutchinson, 2009)

Tony Benn Diaries 1940–2013
   (Hutchinson, published between 1987 and 2013)

House of Commons Official Report (Hansard) 1950–2001

Index